CELESTINA

OR THE TRAGI-COMEDY OF CALISTO AND MELIBEA

Fernando de Rojas

Translated by James Mabbe
and adapted by Eric Bentley

APPLAUSE
THEATRE BOOK PUBLISHERS
211 West 71 St. New York, N.Y. 10023

CELESTINA

Rojas, Fernado de, d. 1541.
   Celestina: or, the tragi-comedy of Calisto and Melibea.
   I. Bentley, Eric, 1916-   . II Title.
PQ6427.E56   1986   862'.2   86-3436

ISBN: 0-936839-01-5

Applause Theatre Book Publishers
211 W. 71st Street
New York, NY 10023
212-595-4735

First Applause Printing, 1986.
Second Applause Printing, 1992.

CELESTINA

DRAMATIS PERSONAE

CALISTO, *a young enamoured gentleman*

MELIBEA, *daughter to Pleberio*

PLEBERIO, *father to Melibea*

ALISA, *mother of Melibea*

CELESTINA, *an old bawd*

PARMENO[1]

SEMPRONIO

TRISTAN, *a page*[1] } *servants to Calisto*

SOSIA

CRITO, *a whoremaster*

LUCRECIA, *maid to Pleberio*

ELICIA

AREUSA } *whores*

CENTURIO, *a ruffian*

THE TIME: *about 1500*
THE PLACE: *a city in Spain*

A note on *thou* and *you*. Most readers will be familiar with the distinction between *tu* and *vous* in modern French. It is a useful distinction to keep in mind when reading the seventeenth-century English of such a text as the present one, though the English—in this matter as in others—are less consistent and therefore less clear.

---

[1] In the Spanish, the first syllable of Parmeno has an accent. Though this is omitted from the present English version, the name should still be stressed on the first syllable. Tristan, on the other hand, is stressed on the second.

ACT I

A garden

CALISTO, MELIBEA

CALISTO. In this, Melibea, I see the greatness of God.

MELIBEA. In what, Calisto?

CALISTO. In endowing thee with so perfect a beauty and in affording me the favour of thy presence—at a place convenient to unsheathe my secret grief. My reward in this is far greater than I have merited by my services to Him. The glorious saints, delighting in the Divine Presence, enjoy no greater pleasure than I, glorified by thy presence!

MELIBEA. Holdest thou this, Calisto, so great a guerdon?

CALISTO. So great that if God should give me a seat above His saints in Heaven, I should not hold it so great.

MELIBEA. I shall give thee a reward answerable to thy deserts if thou persevere in this manner!

CALISTO. O fortunate ears that hear such tidings!

MELIBEA. Unfortunate by the time they hear thy doom! Go, wretch! Begone! My patience cannot endure that a man should presume to speak to me of his delight in illicit love!

CALISTO. I go; but as one against whom adverse Fortune aimeth the extremity of her hate.

CALISTO's house

CALISTO

CALISTO. Sempronio, Sempronio, why Sempronio, I say, where is this accursèd varlet?

Enter SEMPRONIO.

SEMPRONIO. I am here, sir, about your horses.

CALISTO. My horses, you knave, how haps it then that thou comest out of the hall?

SEMPRONIO. The falcon was frisky, and I came in to set him on the perch.

CALISTO. Mischief light upon thee and bring thee (which shortly I hope to see) to a disastrous death! Come, thou unlucky rogue, make ready my bed!

SEMPRONIO. Presently, sir, the bed is ready for you.

CALISTO. Shut the windows, and leave darkness to accompany him whose sad thoughts deserve no light. O death, how welcome art thou to those who outlive their happiness!

SEMPRONIO. What's the matter with you?

CALISTO. Away! Do not speak to me or these hands shall cut off thy days by speedy death!

SEMPRONIO. I will be gone, sir.

CALISTO. The devil go with thee!

SEMPRONIO. There is no reason that he should go with me who stays with you.

He is now outside.

What squint-eyed star hath robbed this gentleman of his wonted mirth—and of his wits? Shall I leave him alone, or shall I go in to him? If I leave him alone, he will kill himself. If I go in, he will kill me. Let him bide alone and bite upon the bit, I care not. Better it is that *he* die whose life is hateful to him than that *I* die when life is pleasing unto me. And say that I should not desire to live save only to see my Elicia, that alone is motive enough to make me look to myself. But admit he should kill himself without any further witness, then must I give account of his life. The safest is to enter.

He goes inside.

CALISTO. Sempronio!

SEMPRONIO. Sir!

CALISTO. Reach me that lute.

SEMPRONIO, *returning.* Sir, here it is.

CALISTO, *singing*.

> Tell me what grief so great can be
> As to equal my misery?

SEMPRONIO. This lute, sir, is out of tune.

CALISTO. How can he tune it, who himself is out of tune? Take this lute and sing me the most doleful ditty thou canst devise.

SEMPRONIO, *singing*.

> Nero from Tarpey doth behold
> How Rome doth burn all on a flame.
> He hears the cries of young and old
> Yet is not grievèd at the same.

CALISTO. My fire is far greater and less her pity whom now I speak of.

SEMPRONIO, *aside*. I was not deceived when I said my master had lost his wits.

CALISTO. What's that, Sempronio?

SEMPRONIO. Nothing, sir.

CALISTO. Tell me what thou saidst: be not afraid.

SEMPRONIO. Marry, I said, how can that fire be greater which but tormenteth one man than that which burnt such a multitude?

CALISTO. What difference there is betwixt shadow and substance, so great is the difference betwixt the fire thou speakest of and that which burneth me. If the fire of Purgatory be like unto this, I had rather my soul should go to oblivion with the beasts than by such means share the glory of the saints.

SEMPRONIO, *aside*. Is it not enough to be a fool but you must also be a heretic?

CALISTO. Did I not tell thee thou shouldst speak aloud?

SEMPRONIO. Are you not a Christian?

CALISTO. I am a Melibean: I adore Melibea, I believe in Melibea, and I love Melibea.

SEMPRONIO, *aside*. My master is all Melibea, whose heart, not able to contain her, like a boiling vessel venting its heat, goes bubbling her name in his mouth!

To CALISTO.

Well, now that I know on which foot you halt, I shall heal you.

CALISTO. Thou speakest of matters beyond the moon. It is impossible.

SEMPRONIO, *aside*. As if Love had bent his bow, shot all his arrows only against him!

CALISTO. Sempronio!

SEMPRONIO. Sir?

CALISTO. Do not go away.

SEMPRONIO. This pipe sounds another tune.

CALISTO. What dost thou think of my malady?

SEMPRONIO. That you love Melibea.

CALISTO. And nothing else?

SEMPRONIO. It is misery enough to have a man's will chained to one place only.

CALISTO. Thou wot'st not what constancy is.

SEMPRONIO. Perseverance in ill is not constancy but obstinacy, so they call it in *my* country.

CALISTO. It is a foul fault for a man to belie that which he teacheth to others: for thou thyself takest pleasure in praising thy Elicia.

SEMPRONIO. Do you the good which I say but not the ill which I do.

CALISTO. Why dost thou reprove me?

SEMPRONIO. Because you subject the dignity of a man to the imperfection of a woman.

CALISTO. A woman? O thou blockhead, she's a goddess!

SEMPRONIO. As goddesses were of old. Have you not heard of Pasiphaë who played the wanton with a bull and of Minerva who dallied with a dog?

CALISTO. Tush, they are but fables.

SEMPRONIO. And that of your grandmother and her ape, that's a fable too? Witness your grandfather's knife that killed the villain who did cuckold him!

CALISTO. A pox of this coxcomb!

SEMPRONIO. Have I nettled you, sir? Oh, many women have been virtuous and noble, but, touching the others, who can recount their falsehoods, their tricks, their tradings, their truckings, their lightness, their tears, their mutabilities and impudencies, their dissemblings, their talkativeness, their deceits, their forgetfulness, their unkindness, their ingratitude, their fickleness, their sayings and gainsayings and all in a breath, their windings and turnings, their vainglory, their coyness, their pride, their base submissions, their prattlings, their gluttony, their sluttishness, their witcheries, their cheatings, their gibings, their slanderings, and their bawdry? They observe no mean; they have no reason; nor do they take any heed in what they do. They will privately pleasure him whom afterwards they will openly wrong; and draw him secretly in at their windows whom in the streets they will publicly rail at. They will give you roast meat, and beat you with the spit. They will invite you unto them, and send you packing with a flea in your ear. And, which is the true humour of a woman, whatsoever her will divines, that must be effected and, be it impossible, yet, not effecting it, she straightway censures your want of wit or affection, if not both. O what a plague! What a hell! Nay, what a loathsome thing it is for a man to have to do with them any longer than in the short prick of time that he holds them in his arms!

CALISTO. The more inconveniences thou settest before me, the more I love her. Who taught thee all this?

SEMPRONIO. Why, they themselves, who no sooner uncover their shame than they lose it. Balance thyself aright in the true scale of thine honour. You are a man endued with wisdom, favour, largeness of limbs, force, and agility of body. Fortune hath in so good a measure shared what is hers with you that your inward graces are by your outward the more beautified, and the stars were so propitious at your birth that you are beloved of all.

CALISTO. But not of Melibea. An thou dost glorify my gifts, I will tell thee, Sempronio, compared with Melibea's, they are but as stars to the sun. Do but consider the nobleness of her blood, the great estate she is born into, the excellency of her wit, the splendour of her virtues, her stately carriage, and, lastly, her divine beauty—whereof, I pray thee, give me leave to discourse a little——

SEMPRONIO, *aside*. What lies will my master tell me now?

CALISTO. What's that?

SEMPRONIO. I said I would have you tell me.

CALISTO. I will begin with her hair. Hast thou seen those skeins of fine gold which are spun in Arabia? Her hair is more fine and shines no less. Daintily combed and knit up in knots with curious ribboning, it has the power to transform men into stones.

SEMPRONIO, *aside*. Into asses, rather.

CALISTO. What sayest thou?

SEMPRONIO. That this could not be asses' hair.

CALISTO. Her eyes are quick, the brows prettily arched, her teeth small and white, her lips red and plump. Her breasts are placed at a fitting height, but their rising roundness and the pleasing fashion of her little tender nipples, who is able to figure forth? So distracted is the eye of man when he beholds them. The proportion of those other parts which I could not eye must undoubtedly (judging things unseen by the seen) be incomparably better than that which Paris gave his judgment of.

SEMPRONIO. Have you done, sir?

CALISTO. As briefly as I could.

SEMPRONIO. In that you are a man, I still say you are more worthy than she.

CALISTO. In what?

SEMPRONIO. In that she is imperfect: out of which defect she lusts and longs after yourself or someone less worthy. Did you never read the philosopher who tells you that as matter desires form, so woman desires man?

CALISTO. When shall I see this between me and Melibea?

SEMPRONIO. It is possible that you may, and as possible that, when you come to the full enjoying of her, you may hate her, looking on her with other eyes.

CALISTO. With what eyes?

SEMPRONIO. With clear eyes.

CALISTO. And with what, I pray, do I see now?

SEMPRONIO. With false eyes, like some kind of mirrors, which make little things seem great, and great little. Do not despair. Myself will take this business in hand.

CALISTO. I am proud to hear thee, though hopeless of obtaining my desire.

SEMPRONIO. Nay, I will assure it to you.

CALISTO. Heaven be thy speed! My cloth-of-gold doublet, it is thine, Sempronio. Take it.

SEMPRONIO, *aside*. I thank you for this and for many more to come. If my master clap such spurs to my side, I doubt not that I shall bring her to his bed. Without reward it is impossible to go through with anything.

CALISTO. Tell me, how dost thou think to purchase her pity?

SEMPRONIO. I shall tell you. It is now a good while since, at the lower end of this street, I fell acquainted with an old bearded woman called Celestina, a witch, subtle as the devil, and well-practised in all rogueries, one who has marred and made up again a hundred thousand maidenheads in this city. Such authority she hath, what by her persuasions and devices, that none can escape her. She will move rocks if she list and at her pleasure provoke them to lechery.

CALISTO. O that I might but speak with her!

SEMPRONIO. I will bring her hither. Use her kindly, and whilst I go my ways, study to express your pains as well as, I know, she is able to give you remedy.

CALISTO. O but thou stayest too long!

SEMPRONIO. I am gone. God be with thee.

Exit SEMPRONIO.

CALISTO. And with thee!

He kneels.

Almighty and Everlasting God, Thou who ledst the Three Kings to Bethlehem with Thy star, most humbly I beseech Thee lead my Sempronio, that he may turn my joy to torment and bring me, all unworthy, to the longed-for goal!

CELESTINA's *house*

CELESTINA, ELICIA, CRITO

CELESTINA. Elicia, what will you give me for my good news?

SEMPRONIO, *outside*. Sempronio is come!

ELICIA. O hush! Peace, peace!

CELESTINA. Why? What's the matter?

ELICIA. Peace, I say, for here is Crito!

CELESTINA. Put him in the little chamber where the besoms be! Quickly, quickly, I say, and tell him a cousin of yours is come!

ELICIA. Crito, come hither quickly, oh, my cousin is come, what shall I do? Come quickly!

CRITO. With all my heart. Do not vex yourself.

Exit CRITO. *Enter* SEMPRONIO.

SEMPRONIO. O my dear mother, I thank my fate that hath given me leave to see you!

CELESTINA. My son, my king, thou hast ravished me with thy presence! Embrace me once more! What? Three whole days and never see us? Elicia, Elicia, wot you who is here?

ELICIA. Who, mother?

CELESTINA. Sempronio, daughter!

ELICIA, *aside*. O how my heart leaps and beats in my body, how it throbs within me!

CELESTINA. Do you see him? I will embrace him; you shall not.

ELICIA, *to* SEMPRONIO. Out, thou accursèd traitor, pox, plagues, and botches consume thee! Die thou by the hands of thine enemies and that for some notorious crime, ay me!

SEMPRONIO. Why, how now, my Elicia, what is it troubles you?

ELICIA. Three days? And in all that time not once come and see me?

SEMPRONIO. Where'er I go, thou goest with me. Where I am,

there art thou. But soft! Methinks I hear somebody's feet above. Who is it?

ELICIA. Who is it? One of my sweethearts!

SEMPRONIO. Nay, like enough.

ELICIA. Nay, it is true, go up and see.

SEMPRONIO. I go.

CELESTINA. Come hither, my son, regard not what she says, for she will tell you a thousand flimflam tales. Come with me and let us talk.

SEMPRONIO. But, I pray, who is that above?

CELESTINA. Would you know who?

SEMPRONIO. I would.

CELESTINA. A wench recommended unto me by a friar.

SEMPRONIO. What friar?

CELESTINA. Well, to save your longing, it is the fat friar.

SEMPRONIO. Alack, poor wench, what a heavy load she is to bear!

CELESTINA. We women must bear all.

SEMPRONIO. Then let me see her.

ELICIA. Wretch! Let your eyes start out of your head and drop down at your feet, for I see it is not one wench that can serve your turn. Go up and see her, but see you come at me no more!

SEMPRONIO. Nay, if this make you so angry, I will neither see her nor any other woman, I will only speak a word with my mother and so bid you adieu.

ELICIA. Go, begone, and stay away three years more if thou wilt!

SEMPRONIO. Mother, put on your mantle, and let us go. By the way I will tell you all.

CELESTINA. Elicia, farewell, make fast the door. Farewell, walls!

Exeunt CELESTINA *and* SEMPRONIO.

A *street*

CELESTINA, SEMPRONIO

SEMPRONIO. Now, mother, let not your ears go a-woolgathering, for he that is everywhere is nowhere. Listen!

CELESTINA. The friendship which hath taken such deep rooting betwixt thee and me needeth no preambles, no circumlocution, no preparation, no insinuation. Be brief!

SEMPRONIO. Calisto is hot in love with Melibea, and, because he needeth our joint furtherance, let us join together to make some purchase of him. For to take occasion by the foretop, why, it is the rung by which many have climbed to prosperity.

CELESTINA. The winking of an eye is enough for me, for, old as I am, I can see day at a little hole. I tell thee, Sempronio, I am as glad of this news as surgeons of broken heads, and, as they go festering the wounds to endear the sore, so will I delay Calisto's winning of Melibea. For the farther he is from effecting, the fairer will he promise to have it effected.

SEMPRONIO. No more. We are now at the gate, and walls, they say have ears.

They have come to CALISTO'S *house.*

CELESTINA. Knock!

SEMPRONIO *knocks.*

CALISTO'S *house*

CALISTO, PARMENO, SEMPRONIO, CELESTINA

CALISTO. Parmeno!

PARMENO. Sir?

CALISTO. What a pox, art thou deaf, canst thou not hear?

PARMENO. What would you, sir?

CALISTO. Somebody knocks. Run!

PARMENO, *shouting through a window*. Who's there?

SEMPRONIO, *shouting back*. Open the door for this matronly dame and me.

PARMENO. It is Sempronio and an old bawd. O how she is bedaubed with painting!

CALISTO. Peace, you villain, she is my aunt. Run and open the door.

Aside.

Thinking to keep this matter from Parmeno, I shall have fallen into the displeasure of a woman who hath no less power over my life than God himself.

PARMENO, *who overhears this*. Believe it not. By this title of bawd is she generally known. If she pass along the streets and someone blurts out, "See where's the old bawd," she turns about, nods her head, and answers with a cheerful look. If she pass by where there be dogs, they bark out this name. The frogs that lie in ditches croak no other tune. Your shoemakers sing this song, your combmakers join with them. Your gardeners, your ploughmen, your reapers, your vine-keepers pass away the painfulness of their labors in making her the subject of their discourse, your gamesters never lose but they peal forth her praises—to be short, all things repeat no other name but this. Not one stone that strikes against another but presently noiseth out: "Old whore!"

CALISTO. Dost thou know her?

PARMENO. A great while ago my mother dwelt in her parish and, being entreated by this Celestina, gave me unto her to wait upon her, though now she knows me not.

CALISTO. What service didst thou do her?

PARMENO. I went into the market place and fetched her vict-uals so that, though I continued but a little while with her, yet I remember everything as if it were yesterday. This honest whore, this grave matron forsooth, had at the very end of the city, close by the waterside, a lone house, half of it fallen down, ill-contrived, and worse furnished. For to get her living, she had six several trades: she was a laundress, a perfumeress, a former of faces, a mender of cracked maidenheads, a bawd, and had some smatch of a witch. Her first trade was a cloak to all the rest, under colour whereof, being withal a piece of a sempstress, many young wenches that were servants came to her house to work, some on smocks, some on other things. Not one of them but brought either bacon, wheat, flour, or a jar of wine, which they could steal from their mistresses, making her house (for she was the receiver) the rendezvous of their roguery. She was a great friend to your students and pages. To these she sold the innocent blood of those poor souls who did adventure their virginities, drawn on by the reparation which she would make them of their lost maidenheads. Nay, she had access with more secluded virgins and would deal with these at the time of early mass or the stations of the cross. Many have I seen of this party enter her house with covered faces and men behind them, barefoot and disguised, to do penance for their sins. She professed herself a kind of physician, skilled in the curing of little children. She would go and fetch flax from one house and put it to spinning in another that she might have freer access unto all. Yet, notwithstanding her trottings to and fro, she would never miss mass nor vespers, nor neglect the monasteries: they were the markets where she made her bargains. And at home she made perfumes, amber, civet, powders, musk and mosqueta, confections to clarify the skin, waters to make the face glister, lip salves, ointments, and a thousand other slibberslabbers, some made of the lees of wine, some of daffodils. She had a trick to refine the skin with juice of lemons, with turpentine, with the marrow of deer. The oils and greases which she used would turn your stomach: as of bears, horses, camels, snakes, cats of the mountain, badgers, hedgehogs and others. For the mending of lost maidenheads, some she holp with little bladders and others she stitched up with the needle. She had also roots hanging there of sea onion and ground thistle. With these she did work wonders, and when the French ambassador came thither, she made sale of one of her wenches for a virgin three several times.

CALISTO. Parmeno, hold thy hand, we make her stay longer than stands with good manners. Let us go, lest she take it ill. But let me entreat thee, Parmeno, that the envy thou bearest to Sempronio be not an impediment to the remedy whereon my life relieth. I esteem as much of thy counsel as of his labour. As brute beasts do labour more bodily than men, for all this we hold them not in the nature of friends. The like differences do I make between thee and Sempronio, and sign myself unto thee for a friend. But, because, in a case so hard, not only all my good but even my life wholly dependeth, it is needful that I arm myself against all casualties. But let us see her who must work our welfare.

CELESTINA *and* SEMPRONIO *have been eavesdropping.*

SEMPRONIO. Celestina, Parmeno aims unhappily!

CELESTINA. Let me alone with Parmeno; I will bring him like a bird to pick bread from my fist. Thou and I will join together, Parmeno shall make a third, and all of us cheat Calisto.

PARMENO *lets in* CELESTINA *and* SEMPRONIO.

CALISTO. O imaged virtue, hope of my desired end, reliever of my torment, resurrection from my death! I here adore the ground whereon thou treadest!

CELESTINA, *aside to* SEMPRONIO. Can fair words make me fatter? Bid him shut his mouth and open his purse.

PARMENO, *aside.* O unhappy Calisto, kneeling to adore the rottenest piece of whorish earth that ever rubbed her shoulders in the stews! He is fallen into a trap and he will never get out.

CALISTO, *to* SEMPRONIO. What said my mother? She thinks I offer words to excuse my reward?

SEMPRONIO. You have hit the nail on the head, sir.

CALISTO. Come then, bring the keys, I will quickly put her out of that doubt.

Exit CALISTO *with* SEMPRONIO.

CELESTINA. I am very glad, Parmeno, that we have lighted on an opportunity wherein I may make known the singular love I bear to thee and the great interest (though undeservedly) thou hast in me. I say *undeservedly* for not a word you said escaped my ear. And not only that which I hear but even the very secrets of thy heart I pierce with the eyes of my understanding. Parmeno, Calisto is lovesick even to the death. And I would have thee know two conclusions that are infallibly true. The first is that every man must love a woman and every woman love a man. The second is that he who loves must be much troubled with the sweet, superexcellent delight which was ordained by God for the perpetuating of mankind. Now my pearl, my poor silly lad, my pretty little monkey face, come hither, you little whoreson, alack how I pity thy simplicity: thou knowest nothing of the world. But thou hast a harsh voice, and by thy grizzled beard it is easily guessed what manner of man thou art. *Pointing below his belt.*

Is all quiet beneath?

PARMENO. As the tail of a scorpion.

CELESTINA. The sting of a scorpion causeth no swelling, while thine causeth one of nine months' duration!

PARMENO *laughs.*

Laughst thou, pocky rogue?

PARMENO. Nay, mother, I love Calisto, tied thereunto by the fidelity of a servant. I see he is out of the right way, and nothing can befall a man worse than to hunt his desire without hope of a happy end, especially he thinking to recover his game by the vain advice of that beast Sempronio—which is as if he should take the broad end of a spade to dig worms out of a man's hand.

CELESTINA. Knowest thou not, Parmeno, that it is folly to bewail that which cannot be holpen? Thou canst not turn the stream of his passion. Tell me, Parmeno, hath not the like happened to others as well as to him?

PARMENO. But I would not have my master languish and grow sick.

CELESTINA. He is not sick and, were he never so sick, the power to make him whole lies in the hands of this weak old woman.

PARMENO. This weak old whore!

CELESTINA. Now the hangman be thy ghostly father! My pretty villain, how dar'st thou be so bold with me?

PARMENO. Marry, I am Parmeno, son to Alberto thy friend, who lived some little while with thee when thou dweltst by the river.

CELESTINA. Good Lord, art thou Parmeno, Claudina's son?

PARMENO. The very same.

CELESTINA. Now the fire of the pox consume thy bones, for thy mother was an old whore as myself! Come hither unto me, come, I say! Many a cuff on the ear have I given thee in my days and many kisses too! Ah, you little rogue, dost thou remember, sirrah, when thou lay'st at my bed's feet?

PARMENO. Passing well. You would take me up to your pillow and there lie hugging of me, and because you savoured somewhat of old age I would fling and fly from you.

CELESTINA. Out, impudent, are you not ashamed! But, to leave jesting: albeit I have made myself a stranger unto thee, yet thou wast the only cause that drew me hither. My son, thou art not ignorant how thy mother gave thee unto me. Thy father died of the grief he suffered for the uncertainty of thy life. And when the time came to leave this world, he sent for me and told me to enquire after thee and bring thee up as mine own: as soon as thou shouldst come to man's estate, I should uncover unto thee a certain place where he hath left thee more gold than all the revenues paid to thy master Calisto. I have spent much time and money enquiring after thee, and never till three days since heard where you abode. And now, my son, return to reason! Settle thyself some place or other! And where better than where I shall advise thee? Continue here and serve this master—but not with foolish loyalty as hitherto thou hast done. The masters of these times love more themselves than their servants, neither in so doing do they do amiss: the like love ought servants to bear unto themselves. My son Parmeno, thy master is one that befools his servants and wears them out to the very stumps. Get thee some friends in his house (for with him thou must not think to fasten friendship where there is such difference of estate). As for that which I told you of, it shall be safely kept; in the meanwhile it shall be much for thy profit that thou make Sempronio thy friend.

PARMENO. My hair stands on end. I hold thee for my mother, Calisto for my master, I desire riches but would not get them wrongfully!

CELESTINA. Marry, sir, but I would. Right or wrong, so as my house may be raised high enough, I care not.

PARMENO. Well, we are of two contrary minds. I would pass through woods without fear, take my sleep without startings. Contented poverty is safe and secure.

CELESTINA. Heaven be thanked thou hast wealth. But the greater a man's fortune, the less secure, and therefore we must arm ourselves with friends. And where canst thou get a fitter, nearer, and better companion tham Sempronio? O Parmeno, what a life might we lead, even as merry as the day is long! Sempronio loves Elicia, kinswoman to Areusa.

PARMENO. To Areusa?

CELESTINA. Ay, to Areusa.

PARMENO. Areusa, the daughter of Eliso?

CELESTINA. Areusa, the daughter of Eliso.

PARMENO. Is this certain?

CELESTINA. Most certain.

PARMENO. It is marvellous strange.

CELESTINA. Dost thou like her?

PARMENO. Nothing in the world more.

CELESTINA. Thou shalt have her. Man, she is thine, as sure as a club.

PARMENO. Nay, soft, mother, give me leave not to believe thee.

CELESTINA. He is in error that will believe no man!

PARMENO. I dare not be so bold.

CELESTINA. Fainthearted is he that ventureth not for his good!

PARMENO. O Celestina, I have heard that a man should converse with those that may make him better. As for Sempronio, by his example shall I not be won to be virtuous, nor shall he by my company be withdrawn from being vicious.

CELESTINA. There is no wisdom in thy words, for without company there is no pleasure in the possession of anything. Delight is with friends, in things that are sensual, but especially in recounting matters of love, the one to the other. "Let us go by night! Hold thou the ladder! Look, where the cuckold her husband goes! Thus did I kiss her! Thus came we nearer!" Is there any delight in all this without company?

PARMENO. I would not, mother, that you should draw me on as those do who draw men to drink of their heresies, sugaring the cup with sweet poison to catch the wills of the weak-minded and blind the eyes of their reason with the powder of sweet-pleasing affection!

CELESTINA. What is reason, you fool? What is affection, you ass? Discretion (which thou hast not) must determine that; and discretion gives the upper hand to prudence; and prudence cannot be had without experience; and experience cannot be found but in old folks, fathers and mothers; and good parents give good counsel, as I do thee, whose life I prefer before mine own.

PARMENO. I am suspicious of this doubtful counsel. I am afraid to venture.

CELESTINA. He that wilfully refuseth counsel shall suddenly come to destruction! And so, Parmeno, I rid myself of thee. *She starts to go.*

PARMENO, *to himself.* What I were best to do I know not. I have heard that a man should believe those whose years carry authority. Now what is it she adviseth me unto? To be at peace with Sempronio. And to peace no man should be opposite. I will therefore hearken unto her. Mother, speak anew unto me, for I will receive thy counsel as a kindness. Command me.

CELESTINA. Parmeno, in seeing thee suddenly conform to reason, methinks I behold thy father here before me! What a man he was! But, hush, I hear Calisto coming and thy new friend, Sempronio.

Re-enter CALISTO *and* SEMPRONIO.

CALISTO, *to* CELESTINA. Receive this poor gift of him who with it offers thee his life.

PARMENO, *aside to* SEMPRONIO. What hath he given her?

SEMPRONIO. A hundred crowns.

PARMENO *laughs.*

Hath my mother talked with thee?

PARMENO. She hath.

SEMPRONIO. How is it then?

PARMENO. As thou wilt. Yet I am still afraid.

SEMPRONIO. I fear me I shall make thee twice as much afraid ere I have done.

CALISTO, *to* CELESTINA. Now, mother, get you home and cheer up your house; then hasten thither and cheer up ours.

CELESTINA. God be with you.

CALISTO. And with you.

Exit CELESTINA.

ACT II

CALISTO, SEMPRONIO, PARMENO

CALISTO. Tell me, my masters, the hundred crowns which I gave yonder old beldam, are they well bestowed?

SEMPRONIO. Exceeding well: for better is the use of riches than the possessing of them. And thus, sir, having told you my mind, let me advise that you return to your chamber where I shall talk further with you.

CALISTO. Methinks, Sempronio, it were better that thou shouldst go along with her and hasten her on.

SEMPRONIO. If I leave you thus alone, you will do nothing but sigh, weep, and take on, shutting yourself up in darkness, seeking new means of thoughtful torment, wherein you cannot escape either death or madness. For the avoiding whereof, get some good company about you. The best remedy against love is not to think on love. Kick not against the prick. Feign yourself to be merry, and all shall be well.

CALISTO. Sempronio my friend (for so thy love makes me style thee), since it grieves thee that I should be alone, Parmeno shall stay with me. Parmeno!

PARMENO. I am here, sir.

CALISTO. But I am not, for I did not see thee. Sempronio, ply her hard, I pray thee!

Exit SEMPRONIO.

Now, Parmeno, what thinkest thou? Thou hast opposed thyself to Celestina to draw me to a detestation of her. And I believe thee. Yet had I rather give *her* an hundred crowns than give another five.

PARMENO. It had been better you had employed your liberality on some present for Melibea herself than to cast away your money upon this old bawd—who minds to make you her slave.

CALISTO. How, fool, her slave?

PARMENO. To whom thou tellest thy secret, to him dost thou give thy liberty.

CALISTO. I would fain know this of thee: whether it be not necessary to have a mediator who may go to and fro with my messages until they arrive at *her* ears of whom to have a second audience I hold it impossible?

PARMENO. Marry, sir, one inconvenience is the cause of another and the door that opens unto many.

CALISTO. I understand not thy purpose.

PARMENO. Your losing of your hawk the other day was the cause of your entering the garden where Melibea was; your entering, the cause that you saw her and talked with her; your talk engendered love; your love brought forth pain; and your pain will be the cause of your growing careless of your body, soul, and goods. And that which grieves me most is that you must fall into the hands of this same trot-up-and-down, this maidenhead-monger, this gadding-to-and-fro bawd, who for her villainies in this kind hath been three times tarred and feathered.

CALISTO. Let them tar and feather her the fourth time too. I care not. Thou art not heartsick as I am, Parmeno.

PARMENO. I should but dissemble with you, sir, if I should not tell you that you lost your liberty when you did first imprison your will.

CALISTO. Unmannerly rascal! What remedy Sempronio brings unto me with his feet, the same dost thou put away with thy tongue! Feigning thyself to be faithful, thou art nothing but a lump of earth; a box filled with the dregs of malice; the inn that gives entertainment to envy; not caring so as thou mayest discredit this old woman, be it by right or by wrong. Sempronio did fear his going and thy staying!

PARMENO. My sharp words are better to stifle violent flames than the soft smoothings of soothing Sempronio. These kindle afresh your flames, which shall never leave burning till they have brought you to your grave.

CALISTO. I am in pain and thou readest philosophy to me! Begone, get forth my horse! See he be dressed! I must pass by the house of my Melibea—or rather of my goddess.

PARMENO, *outside.* Holla, boys!

No one stirs.

I must do it myself, and I am glad it is no worse, for I fear, ere long, we shall come to a worse office than to be boys of the spur. Well, let the world slide.

He gets the horse.

How now, you jade, are *you* neighing too? Is not one hot beast enough in the house, or do you too smell Melibea?

CALISTO, *coming out.* When comes this horse?

PARMENO. Here he is. Sosia was not within.

CALISTO. Hold the stirrup. Open the gate a little wider. If Sempronio come in the meanwhile and the old woman with him, will them to stay, for I will return presently.

CALISTO *rides away.*

PARMENO, *alone.* Go, never to return, and the devil go with you! Celestina and Sempronio will fleece you ere they have done and not leave you one master feather to maintain your flight! Unfortunate that I am to suffer hatred for my truth and receive harm for my service! The world is grown to such a pass that it is good to be bad and bad to be good: I will follow the times and do as other men do. Had I credited Celestina I had not been thus ill-entreated by Calisto. But this shall be a warning to me. Let him destroy, hang, drown, burn himself, and give all that he hath to bawds. I will hold my peace and help to divide the spoil. It is an ancient rule that the best fishing is in troubled waters.

A *street*

SEMPRONIO, CELESTINA

SEMPRONIO, *to himself.* Look what leisure the old bearded bawd takes! How softly one leg comes drawling after another! Now she has her money, her arms are broken!

To CELESTINA.

Well overtaken, mother, you will not hurt yourself by too much haste.

CELESTINA. How now, son, what news with you?

SEMPRONIO. Our patient knows not what he would have. He will have his cake baked before it be dough, and his meat roasted before it be spitted.

CELESTINA. There is nothing more proper to lovers than impatience, especially these new lovers who fly out without once thinking on the harm which the meat of their desire may, by overgorging, occasion them—and their servants.

SEMPRONIO. Servants? Shall *we* be burned with the sparkles which scatteringly fly forth of Calisto's fire? I had rather see him go to the devil. Upon the first discovery of danger, I will not stay with him, no, not an hour. But time will tell me what I shall do, for before his final downfall, like a house that is ready to collapse, he will give some token of his ruin. Every day we see strange accidents. If some should tell you: "Thy father is dead; Granada is taken; Peter is robbed; Inez hath hanged herself," what wouldst thou say, save only that some three days later no wonder will be made of it? All things pass after this manner. Just so will it be with my master's love: the farther it goes on, the more it will slacken. Let us make our profit of him whilst this plea is pending.

CELESTINA. I hold with thee and jump in thy opinion. Yet it is necessary that a good lawyer should follow his client's cause, colour his plea with some show of reason. So shall he not want clients—nor Celestina suitors in cases of love.

SEMPRONIO. Frame it to thine own liking. This is not the first business thou hast taken in hand.

CELESTINA. The first, my son? Few virgins hast thou seen in this city to whom I have not been a broker and holp them to sell their wares. There was not a wench born but I writ her down in my register that I might know how many escaped my net. Can I live by the air? By what do I eat and drink? Find clothes to my back and shoes to my feet? In this city was I born; in it was I bred. He that knows not both my name and my house, thou mayest hold him a mere stranger.

SEMPRONIO. Tell me, mother, what passed betwixt you and Parmeno when I went up with Calisto for the crowns?

CELESTINA. I told him that he should gain more by joining in friendship with us than with all his gay glozings, and that he should not make himself a saint before such an old beaten bitch as myself. I put him in mind of his mother, that he might not set my office at nought, herself having been of the same trade.

SEMPRONIO. Is it long since you first knew her?

CELESTINA. Celestina saw her born and holp to breed her up. His mother and I were nail and flesh, buckle and thong; of her I learned the better part of my trade. Had she lived, I should never have lived to be deceived. She was a faithful friend and good companion. If I brought bread, she would bring meat. If I spread the cloth, she would lay the napkins. She was not foolish, nor proud, as most of your women nowadays are, and I swear she would go barefaced from one end of the city to the other, with her wine jar in her hand, and not one would give her worse word than Mistress Claudina. Everyone would feast her, so great was the affection which they bear her, and she never came home till she had tasted some eight or ten sorts of wine, bearing one pottle in her jar and the other in her belly. Her word was as current as gold: if we found ourselves thirsty, we entered the next tavern and called for a quart of wine, though we had not a penny to pay for it. O Sempronio, were it but cat after kind, and that such were the son as was the mother, assure thyself that thy master should remain without a feather and we without farther care!

SEMPRONIO. How dost thou think to make him thine? He is a crafty subtle fox.

CELESTINA. I will bring him to have Areusa, and make him cocksure ours.

SEMPRONIO. Canst thou do any good upon Melibea? Hast thou any good bough to hang by?

CELESTINA. Melibea is fair; Calisto fond and frank and willing to spend. Money can do anything. It splitteth hard rocks. It passeth over rivers dry-foot . . . This is all I know concerning him and her. Now must I go to Pleberio's house. Sempronio, farewell! For though Melibea stands so high upon her pantofles, yet is she not the first that I have made to stoop. They are all ticklish and skittish, given to wincing and flinging, but, after they are well weighed, they prove good highway jades and travel quietly. You may kill them but never tire them. They curse the cocks because they proclaim it is day; the clocks because they go too fast. They lie prostrate as if they looked after the Pleiades, but when they see the morning star arise, they sigh for sorrow. Above all, note how quickly they change: they endure torment for him whom before they had tormented; they are servants to those whose mistresses they were. If the hinges of their door chance to creak, they anoint them with oil, that they may perform their office without noise. They are enemies of the mean and wholly set upon extremes.

SEMPRONIO. Mother, I understand not these terms.

CELESTINA. A woman either loveth or hated him much of whom she is beloved. If she entertain not his love, she cannot dissemble her hate. And because I know this to be true, it makes me go more merrily to Melibea's house than if I had her fast in my fist already. For I know that, though at the first I must woo her, yet in the end she will be glad to sue to me. Here in this pocket of mine I carry a little parcel of yarn and other trinkets, that I may make my easier entrance, as gorgets, coifs, fringes, nippers, needles, and pins, that, whatsoever they call for, I may be ready provided. This bait shall work my acceptance and hold fast the fish.

SEMPRONIO. Take heed what you do. Her father is noble and
of great power and courage, her mother jealous and furious
—and thou no sooner seen but mistrusted. Melibea is the only
child to them both, and, she miscarrying, miscarrieth all
their happiness, the thought whereof makes me tremble.
Seek not to pluck her wings and come back yourself without your plumes!

CELESTINA. As though thou couldst instruct Celestina in her
trade! Before ever thou wast born, I did eat bread with
crust!

SEMPRONIO. It is the condition of men that what they most
desire they think shall never come to pass: I dread both
thine and my punishment. But I desire profit: I would that
this business might have a good end, not that my master
might thereby be rid of his pain, but that I might be rid
of my penury.

CELESTINA's *house*

CELESTINA, SEMPRONIO, ELICIA

ELICIA. Sempronio come! I will score it up, this is news indeed! What, twice in one day?

CELESTINA. Peace, you fool. We have other thoughts to trouble our heads withal. Tell me, is the house clear? Is the
wench gone that expected the friar?

ELICIA. Gone? Yes, and another come, since she went, and
gone, too.

CELESTINA. Sayest thou so? I hope then she came not in vain?

ELICIA. No, by my fay, for though he came late, yet better
late than never, and little need he to rise early, with Heaven
to help him!

CELESTINA. Hie you quickly to the top of the house and bring
me the oil of serpents which is fastened to the piece of rope
that I brought the other night when it rained so fast. Then
open my chest where the paintings be and you shall find a

paper written with the blood of a bat. Bring it, together with a wing of the dragon whereof yesterday we did cut the claws.

ELICIA, *now upstairs*. It is not here, mother: you never remember where you lay your things.

CELESTINA. Do not feign untruths! Though Sempronio be here, be not you proud of it, for he had rather have me for his counsellor than you for his playfellow! Enter into the chamber where my ointments be and there in the skin of a black cat you shall not fail to find it! And bring down the blood of a he-goat and that little piece of his beard which you yourself did cut off!

ELICIA, *down again*. Lo, here it is. I will go up, and take my Sempronio with me.

Exeunt ELICIA *and* SEMPRONIO.

CELESTINA, *alone*. I conjure thee, thou sad god Pluto, Lord of the Infernal Deep, Emperor of the Damned, Captain General of the Fallen Angels, Prince of those three hellish Furies, Tisiphone, Megaera, and Alecto, Administrator of Styx and Dis with their pitchy lakes and litigious chaos, Maintainer of the flying Harpies with the whole rabblement of frightful Hydras, I, Celestina, thy best-known client, conjure thee by these red letters, by the blood of this bird of night wherewith they are charactered, by the weight of the names and signs in this paper, by the fell poison of those vipers whence this oil was extracted, wherewith I anoint this thread of yarn, come presently to wrap thyself therein and never thence depart until Melibea shall buy it of me and in such sort be entangled that the more she shall behold it, the more may her heart be wrought to yield to my request! Open her heart and wound her soul with the love of Calisto and in so extreme a manner that, casting off all shame, she may unbosom herself to me! Do this and I am at thy command to do what thou wilt! But, if thou do not do it, thou shalt forthwith have me thy capital foe and professed enemy. I shall strike with light thy sad and darksome dungeons. I shall cruelly accuse thy continual falsehoods. And, lastly, with enchanting terms, I shall curse thy horrible name! I conjure thee again to fulfil my command! Once, twice, thrice! And so, presuming on thy great power, I go to her with my thread of yarn wherein I verily believe I carry thyself enwrapped.

A street

CELESTINA

CELESTINA. As I walk, I will weigh what Sempronio feared, for it may be that, if my intent should be found out by Melibea's father, it would cost me little less than my life, either by their tossing me in a blanket or causing me to be cruelly whipped, so that my sweet meats shall have sour sauce and my hundred crowns be purchased at too dear a rate. What shall I do? To go back is not for my profit, and to go on stands not with my safety. If I should go back, what will Calisto think—save only that I have revealed this plot to Pleberio, playing the traitor on both sides that I might gain by both? And if he do not entertain so hateful a thought he will rail upon me like a madman saying: "Out, you old whore, false bawd as thou art, thy promises have not proved effectual! Thou shalt not want punishment nor I, despair!" Of two evils it is wise to incline to the lesser, and therefore I had rather offend Pleberio than displease Calisto. Well then, I will go. Besides, Fortune friendeth those that are valiant. Lo, yonder's the gate. Be of good cheer, Celestina, you have seen yourself in greater danger than this! All divinations are in my favour: of four men that I met by the way, three were Johns, whereof two were cuckolds. Not a dog that hath barked at me. I have not seen any bird of a black feather, neither thrush nor crow. And, which is a better sign of luck than all these, yonder do I see Lucrecia standing at Melibea's gate, that is kinswoman to Elicia. It cannot but go well with us. All is cocksure.

PLEBERIO'S *house*

LUCRECIA, CELESTINA

LUCRECIA. What old witch is this, trailing her tail on the ground? How she sweeps the streets with her gown! What a dust she makes!

CELESTINA, *arriving*. By your leave, sweet beauty.

LUCRECIA. Mother Celestina! You are welcome. I do not remember that I have seen you in these parts this many a day. What wind hath driven you hither?

CELESTINA. Love, my daughter, love and the desire to see my friends and bring commendations from your cousin Elicia, as also to see my old and young mistress whom I have not seen since I went from this end of the town.

LUCRECIA. You make me marvel. You were not wont to stir your stumps unless it were for your profit.

CELESTINA. What greater profit would you have, fool, than a person to comply with her desires? Besides, such women as we never want business, especially myself, who, having the breeding of so many men's daughters, go to see if I can sell a little yarn.

LUCRECIA. Did not I tell you so? You never put in a penny but you take out a pound. But, to let that pass, my old mistress hath begun a web: she hath need to buy and you to sell. Come in and stay awhile; you and I will not fall out.

LUCRECIA *goes upstairs to her mistresses*, ALISA *and* MELIBEA.

ALISA, *above, to* LUCRECIA. Who is that you talk withal?

LUCRECIA. That old woman forsooth with the scotch on her nose who sometimes dwelt hard by here. Do not you remember her that stood on the pillory for a witch? That sold young wenches wholesale? And that hath marred many marriages by setting man and wife at odds?

ALISA. Go to, you fool, tell me her name.

LUCRECIA. Her name (saving your reverence) is Celestina.

ALISA. Now I call her to mind. Go to, you are a wag. She, poor soul, is come to beg of me. Bid her come up.

LUCRECIA, *to* CELESTINA. Aunt, it is my mistress' pleasure you come up.

CELESTINA *comes up.*

CELESTINA. All blessings abide with you, good lady, and your noble daughter! My many griefs have hindered my visiting your house, but heaven knows the sincerity of my heart. Among my many miseries, good lady, the money in my purse grows daily less, so that I have no better remedy than to sell this little parcel of yarn and, understanding by your maid that you had need thereof, it is wholly at your command.

ALISA. If it be such as will serve my turn, I shall pay you well for it.

CELESTINA. Madam, it is as fine as the hair of your head, equal as the strings of a viol, white as a flake of snow. Look you, lady!

ALISA. Daughter Melibea, I will leave this honest woman with you, for it is now high time to go visit my sister. I have not seen her since yesterday, and her page is come to tell me that her sickness is grown worse.

CELESTINA, *aside*. Now does the devil prepare my stratagem by reinforcing this sickness. Be strong, my friend, stand stiffly to your tackling, for now is the time or never!

ALISA. What sayest thou?

CELESTINA. I say: cursed be the devil that your sister's sickness is grown upon her! But, I pray, what is her sickness?

ALISA. A pain in her side that I fear will cost her her life. Recommend her recovery in your prayers!

CELESTINA. As soon as I go hence, I will hie me to the monastery where I have many devout virgins, all of them my friends, upon whom I will lay the charge.

ALISA. Do you hear me, Melibea? Give our neighbour that which is reason for her yarn. And you, mother, I pray hold me excused.

CELESTINA. God pardon you, madam, and I do.

Exit ALISA; *but* CELESTINA *continues to address her.*

You have left me here with very good company: God grant that she may long enjoy her youth, a time wherein more delights are found than in this old, decayed carcass of mine which is a spittlehouse of diseases, an inn of infirmities, a storehold of melancholy, a friend to brangling and brawling, a poor cabin without one bough of shelter, whereinto it rains on all sides.

MELIBEA. Why do you speak so ill, mother, of that which the whole world desireth to enjoy?

CELESTINA. They desire to live to be old, because, by living to be old, they live. Fain would the hen live, for all her pip. But who is he, lady, that can recount to you the discommodities of old age? Those deep furrows in the face, that change in the hair, that fading of fresh colour, that want of hearing, weakness of sight, hollowness in the eyes, sinking of the jaws, toothlessness of the gums, feebleness of legs, slowness in feeding . . . Besides, madam, when all these miseries come accompanied with poverty, all sorrows to this must stoop and strike sail, for I never knew any worse habit than that of hunger.

MELIBEA. So goes the market as it goes with you! The rich will sing another song.

CELESTINA. There is no way so fair but hath some foul. Renown and rest, glory and quietness run from the rich by by-conduits and gutters of subtlety and deceit, which pipes are never perceived because they are bricked over with well-wrought flatteries. A rich man shall never hear the truth. Besides, he lies open to every man's envy, and you shall scarce find one rich man but will confess that it had been better for him to have been in a middling state. For riches make not a man rich, but busy; not a master, but a steward. More are they that are possessed by riches than they that possess their riches. Every rich man hath a dozen of sons or nephews which desire nothing more than to see him underground.

MELIBEA. Tell me, mother, are you not Celestina that dwelt near the river?

CELESTINA. The very same.

MELIBEA. By my fay, you are an old woman. I did not know you, neither should I, had it not been for that slash over your face. Then were you fair: now wonderfully altered.

CELESTINA. Madam, the day will come when you shall not know your face in a glass! I am not so old as you take me to be: of four daughters my mother had, myself was the youngest. I am grown grey before my time.

MELIBEA. Here, Celestina, take your money and farewell. I have taken pleasure in your discourse. Poor soul, you look as if you had eaten nothing all this day!

CELESTINA. Man shall not live by bread alone, nor woman, especially me, who use to be fasting two days together! My whole life is nothing else but to seek trouble to myself by serving of others! Wherefore I will tell you the cause of my coming. We were all undone if I should return and you not know it.

MELIBEA. Acquaint me with all your wants, good mother.

CELESTINA. *My* wants, madam? Nay, others', as I told you, not mine. For all my poverty, I never wanted a penny to buy me bread, not in all the time of my widowhood. Yet let me tell you that when the good man is missing, all other good is wanting, for ill does the spindle move when the beard does not wag above.

MELIBEA. Ask what thou wilt—be it either for thyself or anybody else.

CELESTINA. Most gracious lady, I come from one whom I left sick to the death, who only with one word which should come from your mouth and be entrusted in my bosom—I verily assure myself it will save his life.

MELIBEA. I have not fully comprehended thy meaning. Who is this sick man?

CELESTINA. You cannot choose, lady, but know a young gentleman in this city whose name is Calisto?

MELIBEA. Enough! I will have thee burned, thou enemy to honesty! Fie upon thee, filth! Lucrecia, send her packing!

CELESTINA. This poor gentleman is at the point of death.

MELIBEA. Dost thou think I do not perceive thy drift? Wouldst thou have me soil mine honour to give life to a madman?

CELESTINA. Had I thought that your ladyship would have made this bad construction of the matter, even your own permission would not have emboldened me to speak of Calisto or any man.

MELIBEA. Let me hear no more of this leaper over walls, this hobgoblin, this nightwalker! This is he who saw me the other day and began to court me as if he had not been well in his wits. Advise him, old woman, that the way to have his sickness leave him is to leave off loving! Other answer of me shall be none, nor hope for any!

CELESTINA, *aside.* Troy held out longer, and many fiercer dames have I tamed in my days. Tush, no storm lasteth long.

MELIBEA. Speak out, I pray! Hast thou anything to say in thy excuse? What canst thou demand of me for such a one as he?

CELESTINA. Marry, a certain prayer to St. Apollonia for the toothache. They say your ladyship knoweth it. Also that admirable girdle of yours which is reported to have touched all the relics in Rome and Jerusalem. The gentleman is at death's door with the toothache, and this was the cause of my coming. But, since it was my ill-hap to receive so harsh an answer, let him continue in his pain!

MELIBEA. If this be what thou wouldst have, why wentst thou about the bush with me?

CELESTINA. My simple understanding made me believe that, though my words had been worse than they were, yet would you not have suspected any evil in them.

MELIBEA. I have heard such tales of thy cunning tricks that I know not whether I may believe thy errand was for this prayer.

CELESTINA. Never let me pray again if you can draw any other thing from me though I were put to a thousand torments!

MELIBEA. Thou dost so confidently plead thy ignorance that thou makest me almost ready to believe thee. I will hold my sentence in suspense. Neither would I have thee wonder that I was moved, for two things in thy discourse were sufficient to make me run out of my wits: first, that thou shouldst name this gentleman who presumed to talk with me, then that thou shouldst entreat me for him. But since no harm was intended, I pardon all that is past. To cure the sick is a holy work.

CELESTINA. Ay, and so sick, madam, that you would not judge him the man which in your anger you have censured him to be! By my fay, the poor gentleman hath no ill meaning in his heart. He is endued with thousands of graces: for bounty he is an Alexander; for strength an Hector; he has the presence of a prince; he is fair in his carriage, sweet in his behaviour, and pleasant in his conversation; nobly descended; a great tilter; Hercules had not his courage, Narcissus was not as fair, as he whom one poor tooth so tormenteth.

MELIBEA. How long hath he had it?

CELESTINA. His beauty, madam? Since his birth, madam. He is some three and twenty, for here stands she who saw him born and took him up from his mother's feet.

MELIBEA. I ask thee how long hath he had the toothache?

CELESTINA. Some eight days, madam. But you would think he had had it a year, he is grown so weak. And the best remedy he hath is to take his viol: when he sings thereto the birds listen unto him with a better will than to that musician of old which made the trees and stones to move: had he been born then, Orpheus had lost his prey.

MELIBEA. How angry I am with myself that thou hast endured the distemperature of my enraged tongue, he being ignorant and thou innocent of any ill! I will forthwith fulfil thy request and give thee my girdle, and, if this will not serve the turn, come secretly for the prayer tomorrow morning, for I have not time to write it before my mother comes home.

LUCRECIA, *aside.* I smell a rat. I like not this: "come secretly tomorrow." I fear me she will part with more than words.

MELIBEA. I pray, mother, say nothing to this gentleman of

what hath passed, lest he should think me cruel, sudden, or dishonest.

LUCRECIA, *aside*. All the world cannot save her now.

CELESTINA. Madam, I marvel you should entertain the least doubt of my service. Well, I will go hence with this girdle as merrily as if I saw his heart leaping for joy that you have graced him with so great a kindness.

MELIBEA. I will do more for your patient than this, if need require.

CELESTINA, *aside*. You *must* do more than this, though perhaps you will scarce thank us for it.

MELIBEA. What's that?

CELESTINA. I say, madam, that we thank you for it.

LUCRECIA, *aside*. Here's cat in the pan. What choplogic have we here?

CELESTINA. Daughter Lucrecia, come hither to me.

Aside to her.

You shall have a powder of me (but tell not your mistress) to sweeten thy breath, which is a little of the strongest.

LUCRECIA. A blessing on you! I have more need of this than of my meat.

CELESTINA. And yet, you fool, you will be prating against me! Hold your peace, for you know not what need you may have of me. Do not exasperate your mistress!

MELIBEA. I cannot abide that anybody should speak in my presence and I not have a part therein. What sayest thou to her, mother?

CELESTINA. I entreated her to temper herself in the time of your anger, putting her in mind of the adage: "A fit of anger is but a flash of lightning."

MELIBEA. I commend this gentleman to your care.

CELESTINA. I will haste to see how he does.

MELIBEA. And God go with thee. As thy coming hither hath not done me good, thy going hither cannot do me harm.

ACT III

A street

CELESTINA

CELESTINA, *alone.* I am much bound unto thee, Devil whom I conjured! Well hast thou kept thy word! Cheer up, Celestina, things are half ended when they are well begun! Be merry, old stinkard, frolic with thyself, old wench, for thou shalt get more by this one suit than by soldering of fifteen cracked maidenheads. (A pox on these long petticoats, how they fold themselves about my legs!) How many have missed that nail which myself have hit on the head! What would these young graduates in my art have done? Perhaps have bolted out some foolish word to Melibea, whereby they would have lost as much by their prattling as I have gained by my silence. Experience makes men artists in their profession, and such an old woman as I, who at every little channel holds up her coats, shall prove a proficient in her trade. O girdle, my pretty girdle, let me hug thee a little! I will make thee bring her to me.

Enter SEMPRONIO.

SEMPRONIO, *aside.* Either mine eyes do not match or that is Celestina. How her skirts trouble her! Who did ever see her walk the streets before with her head hanging in her bosom and her eyes cast down?

To her.

Good mother! Tell me what news you bring. Is it a son or a daughter? Ever since one of the clock I have waited for you.

CELESTINA. Sempronio, my friend, this is no fit place to tell thee, for by communicating myself to many, I should, as it were, deflower my embassage, whose maidenhead I mean to bestow on your master. Go along with me to Calisto, for though you shall have your parcel of the profit, I mind to have all the thanks for my labour.

SEMPRONIO. "Though you shall have your parcel." I tell you plainly, I do not like this word, that I do not. Parcel me no more of your parcels!

CELESTINA. Go to, you fool, be it part or parcel, man, thou shalt have what thou wilt! What is mine is thine! Hang all this trash rather than that thou and I should fall out about dividing the spoil! Yet old folks have more need than young, especially you, who live at full table upon free cost.

SEMPRONIO. There goes more to a man's life than eating and drinking!

CELESTINA. Ay, a hat, or a stonebow to go shooting at birds, aiming with your eye at other birds that take their stand in windows! There is no better bawd than a stonebow. But woe unto her who is to uphold her credit and begins to grow old as I do!

SEMPRONIO, *aside*. It had been better for me to have fled from this viper than to put her in my bosom. But let her gain what she can gain. I will keep my word with her.

CELESTINA. What sayest thou?

SEMPRONIO. You told me you would defer this business, leading my master along in a fool's paradise, and now you run headlong to tell Calisto of all that passed. Know you not that men esteem those things most which are most difficult to achieve?

CELESTINA. A new business requires new counsel, and various accidents, various advice; nor did I think, son Sempronio, that Fortune would have befriended me so soon. I know that my master is liberal and somewhat of a womanish longing and therefore will give more for one day of good news than for a hundred wherein he is pained. Peace, you fool, let me alone with him!

SEMPRONIO. Then tell me what passed, for I long as much to know that lady's answer as my master doth.

CELESTINA. Peace, you fool! What, does your colour change? Come, I prithee, your master will be ready to run mad.

CALISTO'S *house*

CALISTO *and* PARMENO, *inside*
SEMPRONIO *and* CELESTINA, *outside*

PARMENO. Master! Master!

CALISTO. What's the matter, fool?

PARMENO. I see Sempronio and Celestina coming. And at every step they make a stop, and where they stand, Sempronio, with the point of his sword, makes lines in the ground.

CALISTO. Thou careless, absurd ass, canst thou descry land and not make to the shore? Dispatch, I say! Unbolt the troublesome door, that this honourable woman may enter, in whose tongue lies my life!

CELESTINA, *to* SEMPRONIO. Dost thou hear him? These words are of another tune than those we heard at our first coming hither. The matter, I see, is amended. Never a word shall I tell him but shall be better to old Celestina than a new petticoat.

CELESTINA *and* SEMPRONIO *go inside.*

CALISTO'S *house. Indoors*

On one side, CALISTO *and* CELESTINA
On another, PARMENO *and* SEMPRONIO

CALISTO. Mother! Speak!

CELESTINA. How is it with you, my lord and master? And how can you make this old woman amends, who hath hazarded her life in your service? The very thought whereof empties my veins of all their blood. I would have given my life for less than the price of this old mantle of mine.

PARMENO. Thou art all, I see, for thyself. Thou art like a lettuce that grows between two coleworts: if thou be let alone, thou wilt overtop them. The next I look for is that she beg a kirtle for her mantle. How craftily does she pitch her nets to catch me and my master, seeking to make me faithless and him foolish! Mark her, Sempronio, she will not demand any money of my master, because it is divisible.

SEMPRONIO. Peace, thou despairful fellow, lest Calisto kill thee!

CALISTO. Good mother, either cut off thy discourse, or take this sword and kill me!

PARMENO. He cannot stand. He quivers like one touched with quicksilver. He cannot live long if this fit continue. Every man his mourning weed, and there an end.

CELESTINA. What? Take your sword and kill you? Let your sword kill your enemies. As for me, I will give you life, man, by the good hope I have in her whom you love.

CALISTO. Good hope?

CELESTINA. Ay, good hope, and well may it be called so, since the gates are open for my return: she will sooner receive *me* in this poor tattered kirtle than others in cloth of gold!

PARMENO. Sempronio, sew up this mouth, I can no longer hold.

SEMPRONIO. So she beg her apparel, what's that to thee? I commend her for it.

PARMENO. In one day this old jade would cast off her rugged hairs and get her a new coat—which is more than she could do these fifty years!

SEMPRONIO. Is this all the good she taught thee in breeding you up?

PARMENO. I could be content that she should pill and poll, ask and have, but not cut out all the cloth for her own coat.

SEMPRONIO. It is her fault, I confess. But other vice hath she none. Let her thatch her own house, then afterwards shall she board ours; else had it been better for her she had never known us.

CALISTO. Tell me what she was doing! How gottest thou into the house? How was she apparelled? How did she look on thee?

CELESTINA. With such a look as your fierce bulls use towards those that cast sharp darts against them!

CALISTO. Be these thy good hopes? Death itself could not be half so deadly!

SEMPRONIO. He hath not the patience to stay to hear that which so earnestly he hath desired.

PARMENO. Now, sir, who talks now? Did my master hear you, he would cudgel you!

SEMPRONIO. I offend not him; thou speakest prejudicially of all. Contentious, envious, accursèd caitiff, is this the friendship thou hast contracted with Celestina and me?

CALISTO. All that I have heard are rather tokens of hate than of love. If thou wilt not that I die desperate, certify me briefly whether thy glorious demand had a happy end!

CELESTINA. The greatest glory which is given to the bee (which little creature the discreeter sort ought to imitate) is that whatsoever he toucheth he converteth into a better substance. In like manner hath it befallen me with Melibea: all her sour looks I turned into honey. What did you think Celestina went thither for unless it were to be your shield and buckler and receive upon my mantle all the blows that were struck at you, those revilings and disdainful terms which such as she make show of when they are first sued unto for their love? And why forsooth do they this? To the end that what they give may the better be esteemed. If everyone should say yea as soon as she is asked, there would be no difference between the love of a common whore and an honest damsel that stands upon her honour. And therefore, when they see a man loves them, though they themselves fry in the flames of love, yet they will show a coldness and pour forth words as sharp as vinegar. But because I would have thee take some ease of thy sorrows while I relate all that passed between her and me, know for thy comfort that the end of her discourse was good.

CALISTO. Now my veins recover their lost blood! Now do I find some joy! Sit you down, dear mother, whilst on my knees I give ear to thy sweet answer. Say on, and tell me by what means thou gottest into the house!

CELESTINA. By selling a parcel of thread—by which trick I have taken, in my days, more than thirty such, and some higher women than herself!

CALISTO. Taller, perhaps, but not higher in birth, beauty, discretion, virtue, speech!

PARMENO. Mark how the fool's clock goes: it never strikes under twelve, the finger of his dial is still upon high noon! And, Sempronio, you stand gazing like a wide-mouthed, drivelling fool, hearing his fooleries and her lies!

SEMPRONIO. Say they are but fables she tells him, yet, were it only that her discourse is of love, thou oughtst to heed it. Why shouldst thou alone stop thy ears at that to which all the world is willing to hearken?

CELESTINA. When I was about to sell my thread, Melibea's mother was called away. She left Melibea with me to conclude the bargain.

CALISTO. O singular opportunity! O that I had lain hid under thy mantle that I might have heard her speak!

CELESTINA. Under my mantle, sir? Alack, she must needs have seen you through at least thirty holes—should not Fortune give me a better!

PARMENO. I will get me gone. Sempronio, hear you all for me. The fool measures how many steps there be between this and Melibea's house. All his faculties are possessed with her. But he will find that my counsel would have done him more good than the cunning cozenage of Celestina.

CALISTO, *calling to* PARMENO *and* SEMPRONIO. You keep a-tattling and a-prattling there! As you love me, hold your tongues, and you will die with delight, such pleasure will you take in this repetition! Go on, mother, what didst thou do when thou wast left alone with her!

CELESTINA. I was overjoyed!

CALISTO. So is it now with me. But, tell me, wast thou not stricken dumb with this sudden accident?

CELESTINA. No, but grew thereby the bolder, and opened the very bowels of my heart, told her in what pain you lived, and how that one word from her would ease you of your

torment. But she cut off my words and struck herself a blow
on the breast, charging me to cease my prattle and get me
out of her sight unless I would her servants should make
short work of me, calling me witch, sorceress, bawd, old
whore, false baggage, bearded miscreant, mother of mischief . . . Then fell she into swoonings and trances, her
hands and fingers being clenched one within another, hurl-
ing and rolling her eyes on every side, striking the hard
ground with her tender feet, being wounded with that
golden shaft which, at the very voicing of your name, had
struck her to the heart! I, all this while, stood me still in a
corner like a cloth that is shrunk in the wetting, and the
more her throbs and pangs were, the more did I laugh in
my sleeve, because I knew her yielding would be the sooner
and her fall the nearer. Yet must I tell you that, whilst her
anger did foam out its froth, I did not suffer my thoughts
to run a-woolgathering but took hold on Time's foretop, and
found a salve to heal that hurt which myself had made.

CALISTO. I did dream it would come to this but, dear mother,
I do not see how thou couldst light upon a fit excuse to
cover and colour the suspicion of thy demand.

CELESTINA. I told her your torment was the toothache, and
that that which I craved of her was a prayer.

CALISTO. So high a means of help! O cunning creature! Speedy
remedy!

To PARMENO *and* SEMPRONIO.

What think you now, my masters? Was ever the like woman
born in this world?

CELESTINA. Give me leave to continue, for night draws on, and
I would not go home in the dark.

CALISTO. You shall have torches, you shall have pages; make
choice of whom you will to accompany you!

PARMENO. For she is young and handsome and may be ravished by the way. Sempronio, thou shalt go with her because she is afraid of the crickets which chirp in the dark.

CALISTO, *to* PARMENO. What's that, my son?

PARMENO. I said that it were meet that I and Sempronio accompany her home, for it is dark.

CALISTO. Well said, Parmeno.

To CELESTINA.

Proceed, good mother: what answer made she for the prayer?

CELESTINA. Marry, that with all her heart I should have it.

CALISTO. How gracious and how great a gift, O God!

CELESTINA. I craved more than this.

CALISTO. What, mother?

CELESTINA. Her girdle which she wore about her, affirming that it would allay your pain because it had touched so many relics.

CALISTO. What said she?

CELESTINA. Reward me for my news, and I will tell.

CALISTO. Take my house and all that is in it or what thou wilt!

CELESTINA. Give this poor old woman a mantle, and I will give thee her girdle.

CALISTO. A mantle? Tut, a mantle, a kirtle, all I have!

CELESTINA. A mantle shall content me.

CALISTO. Parmeno, call hither my tailor, and let him cut her a mantle and kirtle of fine, pure cloth!

PARMENO, *aside*. I may go hang myself when I have done, whilst the old woman with a pox will have every day change of raiment.

CALISTO. Envious wretch, what mumblest thou to thyself? Get thee gone with a murrain! There will as much of the cloth be left to make thee a jerkin.

PARMENO. I said nothing, sir, but that it is too late to have the tailor come tonight.

CALISTO. Then let it alone till tomorrow. Now, mother, I pray, let me see this glorious girdle that my afflicted heart may rejoice therein. All my senses have been wounded by her— the eyes in seeing her, the ears in hearing her, the hands in touching her.

CELESTINA. What? You have touched her?

CALISTO. In my sleep.

CELESTINA. Oh, in your dreams?

CALISTO. I have seen her so oft in my dreams, I fear that will happen unto me which befell Alcibiades—he dreamed he saw himself enwrapped in his mistress' mantle, and was the next day murdered.

CELESTINA. Take this girdle and, if death prevent me not, I will deliver into your hands the owner thereof.

CALISTO. O happy girdle, glory of my soul, encircler of so incomparable a creature——

SEMPRONIO. Sir, it is not your rejoicing in this girdle that can make you to enjoy Melibea.

CALISTO. Yet have I not the power to abstain from adoring so great a relic.

CELESTINA. She gave you this for to ease your toothache, not for love.

CALISTO. And the prayer thou hast talked of?

CELESTINA. She hath not given it me yet.

CALISTO. Why not?

CELESTINA. The shortness of time. She willed me to return tomorrow if your pain do not decrease.

CALISTO. Decrease! My pain shall decrease when I see a decrease of her cruelty.

CELESTINA. Sir, she will yield you any help which I shall crave at her hands. Tell me, I pray, if this be not well for the first bout? Well, I will get me home, and have a care, if you walk abroad, that you go muzzled about the cheeks with a cloth that she, seeing you, may not accuse me of falsehood.

CALISTO. I will not stick to clap on four cloths! But passed there nothing more between you? I long to hear the words which flow from so sweet a mouth! How didst thou dare, not knowing her, to be so bold?

CELESTINA. Not knowing her? They were my neighbours four years together. Her mother knows me better than her own hands, and Melibea, too, though now she be grown so great a lady.

PARMENO. Sempronio, a word in your ear.

SEMPRONIO. What's the matter?

PARMENO. Give her a touch on the toe that she may be gone.

CALISTO. Was her like ever born into the world? Did God ever create a better body? If Helen were now alive she would do reverence to this lady for whom I languish!

CELESTINA, *to* SEMPRONIO, *who has approached her.* I understand. But give him leave to run on, for he will fall from his ass, and his journey be at an end.

CALISTO. Nothing could be added to make her fairer! A little fountain water with a comb of ivory is sufficient to make her surpass all other of her sex!

CELESTINA. Sir, give me licence to take my leave of you, for it grows late. And let me have the girdle: I must use it.

CALISTO. Alack, with thee or with this girdle or with both, I would willingly have been accompanied all the dark and tedious night, but there is no perfect happiness in this life. Where be my men? Parmeno, I say!

PARMENO. Here, sir.

CALISTO. Accompany this matron to her house.

CELESTINA. Tomorrow I shall return, not doubting but my mantle and her prayer shall meet here together. Be patient. Settle your thoughts upon other things.

CALISTO. Impossible! It were heresy to forget her for whom alone my life pleaseth me!

A street

PARMENO, CELESTINA

CELESTINA. Parmeno, I ever held thee to be my son and thought thou wouldst have showed thyself more loving to me, but thou gavest me bad payment, even to my face, whispering against me in the presence of Calisto. But mark: an old woman is a help, a comforter, an inn to give rest to a sound man, a hospital to cure a sick man, a fire in winter, shade in summer, a tavern to eat and drink in. What sayest thou, my pretty fool? I know thou art ashamed of that which thou hast spoken today. Thou canst not say B to a battledore, thou art struck so dumb and dead. And therefore I will not crave any more at thy hands than that which friendship craves of thee, which is: look upon Sempronio. Next under heaven, myself have made him a man. I could wish you would live and love together as brothers and friends. If you will be beloved, you must love, you know: trouts cannot be taken with dry breeches, and if the cat will have fish she must wet her foot.

PARMENO. Mother, I confess the one fault, and offer myself to be ordered by you in all future proceedings, but it is impossible that I should hold friendship with Sempronio. How is it possible to make a contract betwixt two such contrary natures?

CELESTINA. You two are equals; and parity of persons is the main prop of friendship. Take heed, my son: be wise to gain more, for one fortune is gained already. What pains your father took to gain it! But I may not put it into your hands till you lead a more reposed life.

PARMENO. What do you call a reposed life, mother?

CELESTINA. Marry, son, to live of yourself! Not to set thy foot under another man's table, which thou must do unless thou learn to profit of thy service. Out of pity to see thee thus tattered did I beg that mantle of Calisto, thou being without a jerkin. O Parmeno, how happy should I be might I but see thee and Sempronio agree—that you may come to my poor house and each be merry with his wench!

PARMENO. His wench, mother?

CELESTINA. Ay, his wench.

PARMENO. Howbeit I spake against you today, it was not because I thought ill of that which you said, but because, when I told my master the truth, he ill-treated me. Therefore, let us shake hands and use him accordingly. Now I bless the time when you bred me up!

CELESTINA. Son, no more! Mine eyes run over. Thy mother! She was dearer to me than mine own sister. How lusty she was, how quick, how neat, how portly and majestical! Why, she would go you at midnight from churchyard to churchyard seeking for the implements of our trade as if it had been day! She did not omit Christians, Moors, or Jews: by day she would watch them and by night she would dig them out. And one thing I shall tell thee, though I was about to keep it in: she did pull seven teeth out of a fellow's head that was hanged with a pair of pincers such as you pull out stubbed hairs withal, whilst I did pull off his shoes. The very devils did live in fear of her. She was well known to them all, as the beggar knows his dish. One devil came tumbling in upon the neck of another as fast as it pleased her to call them up, and none durst tell her a lie. Since she died, I could never attain to the truth of anything!

PARMENO, *aside.* Accursed be this woman with her wordy phrases!

CELESTINA. What sayest thou, my more than son?

PARMENO. Tell me, when the Justice sent officers to apprehend you—at which time I was in your house—was there any acquaintance between you?

CELESTINA. Any acquaintance? Our cases were alike. They took us, accused us, punished us alike, which was the first punishment we ever had. I wonder that thou shouldst remember it.

PARMENO. True: the worser part of wickedness is the perseverance therein.

CELESTINA, *aside.* He hath pricked me to the quick! But I will tickle him on the right vein.

PARMENO. What say you?

CELESTINA. Marry, son, that, besides this, your mother was taken four times alone; and once she was accused for a witch. She was found one night with certain candles in her hand, gathering I know not what earth at a crossway, for which she stood upon a scaffold with a high paper hat painted full of devils whereon her fault was written, being brought thither through the streets upon an ass. For all this she would not give over her old occupation, which I thought good to tell you, touching that opinion of yours about perseverance. When she was on the scaffold, everyone might see that she cared not a button for those that stood staring upon her. Wherein I thought fit to show you that they who

have anything in them fall more easily into error than any
other. Do but weigh what manner of man the poet Virgil
was. And he was hung out of a tower in a wicker basket,
all Rome looking on. Yet was he not the less honoured.

PARMENO. But this was not enjoined by a Justice!

CELESTINA. Peace, you fool, thou art ignorant what a coarse
kind of justice was executed upon thy mother, how wrongfully, by suborning of false witnesses, and by cruel tortures,
they forced her to confess that which was not! But, being a
woman of great spirit, of all this she reckoned not a pin, saying: "If I broke my leg, it was for my good: it made me
better known than I was before!"

PARMENO. Talk of our present business. You promised me I
should have Areusa.

CELESTINA. Let us walk towards her house. This is the least
that I will do for thee.

PARMENO. I was out of hope ever to have her. It is an ill sign
for a man to see his mistress flee and turn the face. This
did much dishearten me.

CELESTINA. Now shalt thou see what power I have over these
wenches! But, hush, here's the door, let us enter with quiet
steps that the neighbours may not hear us. Stay for me at
the stairs' foot whilst I see what I can do.

AREUSA's *house*

AREUSA, CELESTINA

AREUSA. Who's there? That at this time of night comes up to
my chamber?

CELESTINA. One that is more mindful of you than of herself!

AREUSA, *aside*. Now the devil take this old trot!

To CELESTINA.

What news, that you come stealing like a ghost so late? I
was even putting off my clothes to go to bed.

CELESTINA. So soon to roost? Think you ever to be rich if you go to bed so timely? Come, walk a turn or two and talk with me a little.

AREUSA. How cold it is! I will put on my clothes again.

CELESTINA. By my fay shall you not! But if you will go into your bed, do, and *so* shall we talk.

AREUSA. Yes indeed, I have need to do so, for I have felt very ill all this day.

CELESTINA. Cover yourself well, and sink lower, so shall you be warm. How like a siren you look, how fair, how fresh! What sheets, what quilts, what pillows, how white they be! It does me good to touch you!

AREUSA. Nay, do not touch me, it increaseth my pain.

CELESTINA. What pain, pretty chuck? You jest.

AREUSA. A pain which, rising in my breast, swells up to my throat and is ready to stifle me!

CELESTINA. Give me leave to touch you and I will try what I can do, for I know something for this evil—which everyone calls the Mother.

AREUSA. Lay your hand higher—above the stomach.

CELESTINA. So plump, so clear, so fragrant, so dainty a creature! That any sickness should dare to usurp over such an unparalleled beauty! But it is not so. Your disease is self-conceited, and you are to blame if it be so. You should not lose the flower of your youth under six linings of linen. And do not think you were born for nothing, for when you were born, man was born, and when man was born, woman was born. Nothing was created superfluous.

AREUSA. Give me something for my evil, and leave jesting.

CELESTINA. For this common complaint, every strong scent is good, as of partridge feathers, rosemary, and the soles of old shoes, but there is another thing that I ever found to be better, but what it is I will not tell you as you make yourself such a piece of niceness.

AREUSA. As you love me, mother, tell me!

CELESTINA. You understand me. Do not make yourself more fool than you are.

AREUSA. You know that my lover went yesterday with his captain to the wars: would you have me wrong him?

CELESTINA. Great wrong, I promise you!

AREUSA. Yes, for he supplies my wants, loves me, uses me with respect!

CELESTINA. You can never recover by living sole and simple as you now do.

AREUSA. It is late, mother. Tell me, pray, what wind drove you hither?

CELESTINA. Parmeno complains that you refuse to see him. What should be the reason I know not, unless because you know I wish him well. I regard your friends in a kinder fashion.

AREUSA. Aunt, I am beholding to you.

CELESTINA. I must believe works: for words are wind and are sold everywhere for nothing. Love is paid with love, and works with works. Elicia, thy cousin, is kept in my house by Sempronio. Parmeno and he are companions. Both serve the gentleman you wot of and by whom you may gain great good. Do not deny him that, the granting whereof will cost you so little. See how pat all things fall! To tell you truly, I have brought him along. How say you? Shall I call him up?

AREUSA. Heaven forbid! Ay me! I fear he hath heard every word.

CELESTINA. Entertain him friendly, and, if you think fit, let him enjoy you—and you him, and both one another.

AREUSA. Mother, you know to whom I am bound to give an account. If he know I play false, he will kill me. My neighbours are malicious and will acquaint him therewith.

CELESTINA. For this fear of yours myself have already provided: we entered very softly.

AREUSA. Tush, were it but for one night, I would not care: I speak for many other that are to come.

CELESTINA. What? Is this your fashion? An you use these niceties you shall never have a double room but live like a beggar all the days of your life. Did you but see your cousin's wisdom, you would be of another mind. She does all that I will have her do. She will sometimes boast that she hath at one time had one in bed with her, another waiting at the door, and a third sighing for her within the house; and hath given satisfaction to them all. And are you afraid who have but two to deal withal? Can one cock fill all cisterns? One conduit-pipe water all your court? It goes hard with the mouse that hath but one hole to trust to. One swallow makes not a summer. To feed always upon one dish brings a loathing to the stomach. What would you do, daughter, with this number of one? Two is commendable company as you may see in yourself that hath two ears, two feet, and two hands. The more Moors, the better market. Son Parmeno, come up!

AREUSA. I am ready to swoon! Nay fie, mother, I have no acquaintance with him! I am ashamed!

CELESTINA. I will quit you of this shame, and speak for you both, for he is as bashful as you.

Enter PARMENO.

PARMENO. Gentlewoman, heaven preserve your gracious presence!

AREUSA. You are welcome, gentle sir.

CELESTINA, *to* PARMENO. Whither go you now, to sit moping in the corner? Hearken, both of you. Friend Parmeno, you know what I promised you and you, daughter, know what I entreated at your hands.

To AREUSA.

He hath lived in great pain for your sake, and therefore it shall not be amiss that he stay with you here this night.

AREUSA. For my maidenhead's sake, mother, let it not be so!

PARMENO, *aside to* CELESTINA. Offer her all that my father left with you for me.

AREUSA. What doth this gentleman whisper?

CELESTINA. He says that he is glad of your friendship. He also says that he will be a friend to Sempronio and will do what is needful in a business which we have in hand with his master. Is that not true, Parmeno? Have I your promise?

PARMENO. You have, mother.

CELESTINA, *aside*. So, sir rascal, I have thee now, and in good
time withal! *Aloud*. Come hither, you clown, you clodpoll,
you, I would fain see what thou art worth before I depart.
Roll her on this bed!

AREUSA. He will not be so uncivil!

CELESTINA. Dost thou think, daughter, that I know not what
thing this is? Did I never see a man and a woman together
before? Know I not all their tricks and devices, what they
say and what they do?

AREUSA. Rather would I lose an eye than offend thee. Go thou
but apart a little, and he may do his will.

CELESTINA. I am not angry, look you, I tell you this against
another time. And so good night. I pass my word that you
shall rise tomorrow in good health! And this is a brave fellow, a fighting cock that will not lower his crest after three
nights of the sport! The doctors of my country were wont
to send me such to eat at a time when I had better teeth.
The taste is in my mouth to this day. God be with you.

AREUSA. And with you, aunt.

PARMENO. Shall I accompany you home?

CELESTINA. No, marry, it needs not: I am past all danger of
ravishing.

Exit CELESTINA.

AREUSA's *house*

PARMENO, AREUSA

PARMENO. It is light in the chamber. It is day.

AREUSA. Sleep, sir, and take your rest, for it is but even now
since we lay down. I have scarce shut mine eyes yet and
would you have it to be day? Open the window and you
shall see.

PARMENO. I saw the light come through the chinks of the door.

Aside.

O what a villain I am! Into how great a fault am I fallen with my master.

To AREUSA.

How late in the day it is!

AREUSA. Late?

PARMENO. Late, late in the day.

AREUSA. Alas, I am not eased of the Mother yet; it pains me still.

PARMENO. What wouldst thou have me do, dear love?

AREUSA. Talk a little—of my indisposition.

PARMENO. What, should we talk yet more? It is now high noon. If I stay longer I shall not be welcome to my master. Tomorrow is a new day, and I will come again, and as often afterwards as you please. In the meanwhile, come and dine with us today at Celestina's house.

AREUSA. With all my heart. And farewell. Pull the door after you.

PARMENO. Fare you well.

A *street*

PARMENO

PARMENO. O singular joy! What man lives that can say he is more fortunate than I, more happy, more successful—that I should enjoy so curious a creature! And no sooner ask than have! If I could brook the old woman's treasons, I would creep upon my knees to do her kindness. How shall I requite her? And to whom shall I impart my joy? For it is true, what the old woman told me: Pleasure not communicated is no pleasure. Yonder is Sempronio at our door.

CALISTO'S *house*

SEMPRONIO, PARMENO

SEMPRONIO. What should be the cause of thy so long stay, unless it were to rub old Celestina's feet as thou wast wont to when little?

PARMENO. O Sempronio, my good friend, do not soil with troubled water the clear liquor of my gladsome thoughts! Embrace me with joy, and I shall tell thee wonders!

SEMPRONIO. Out with it, come! Hast thou seen Melibea?

PARMENO. As though all the world were enclosed in Melibea!

SEMPRONIO. Then we are all in love: Calisto loves Melibea; I love Elicia; and thou, out of mere envy, hast found someone with whom to lose thy little wit.

PARMENO. Do not torment me, Sempronio, with wounding words. Who lives there that sees himself, as I have, raised to the height of my dear Areusa's love? And who, that sees himself more likely to fall from thence than I, being so ill treated of thee? Thou wilt not give me leave to tell thee how much I am thine, what good counsel I received of Celestina and all for thy good and the good of us all. And now that we have our master's and Melibea's game in our hands, now is the time that we must thrive or never!

SEMPRONIO. Thou knowest Areusa, that is cousin to Elicia?

PARMENO. I did enjoy her.

SEMPRONIO. What dost thou call enjoying her? Did she show herself at a window?

PARMENO. I left her in doubt whether she be with child.

SEMPRONIO. The old woman had a finger in this business, had she not?

PARMENO. Her little finger. O brother, what shall I say unto thee of the graces of that wench?

SEMPRONIO. She is cousin to Elicia. But what did she cost thee?

PARMENO. Not anything. So rich an object was never purchased at so low a rate. I have invited her to dinner at Celestina's house. Let us all meet there.

SEMPRONIO. Who?

PARMENO. Thou and she, and the old woman and Elicia.

SEMPRONIO. Now I long to embrace thee! The hatred which I bare thee is turned into love. Let us live like brothers! Let us feast and be merry, for our master will fast for us all!

PARMENO. What does the desperate man?

SEMPRONIO. Lies where thou hast left him last night upon his pallet by his bedside like a man in a trance between sleeping and waking. If I go in to him, he falls a-routing and a-snorting. If I go from him, he either sings or raves. Nor can I comprehend whether the man be in pain or ease.

PARMENO. Did he never call for me? Did he not remember me?

SEMPRONIO. Why should he remember thee? He remembered not himself.

PARMENO. Since things go well, I will send thither our meat. We have wine of Monviedro in the larder, a gammon of bacon, and some dozen dainty chickens which my master's tenants brought the other day and the turtle doves which he willed me to keep against today—I will tell him that they stank and I threw them away. And we will talk with the old woman concerning his love—to his loss and our profit.

SEMPRONIO. Callest thou it love? I verily think he will hardly escape either death or madness.

CALISTO, *in another room.*

> In peril great I love
> And straight of force must die
> Since what desire doth give
> That hope doth me deny.

PARMENO. Our master is a-rhyming, he is turned poet.

SEMPRONIO. The great poet Ovid who never speaks but in verse! Pshaw, he does but talk in his sleep.

CALISTO, *indoors.*

> This pain, this martyrdom,
> O heart, well dost thou prove

Since thou so soon wast won
To Melibea's love.

PARMENO. Did I not tell thee?

CALISTO. Who talks in the hall, ho!

PARMENO. Anon, sir.

PARMENO and SEMPRONIO go in to him.

CALISTO. Is it time to go to bed?

PARMENO. It is, rather, sir, too late to rise.

CALISTO. Is the night past and gone?

PARMENO. Ay, and a good part of the day too.

CALISTO. Give me my clothes. I must go to St. Mary Magdalen's and ask God to direct Celestina and put my remedy into Melibea's heart or else shorten my sorrowful days!

SEMPRONIO. Good sir, leave off these poetical fictions, and eat some conserves that you may keep some life in you.

CALISTO. Sempronio, loyal follower, be it as thou wilt have it, for I assure myself that my life is as dear unto thee as thine own.

SEMPRONIO, *aside to* PARMENO. If thou goest for the conserves, steal a barrel for those thou knowest of.

CALISTO. What sayest thou?

SEMPRONIO. I speak, sir, to Parmeno that he should fetch you a slice of conserves.

PARMENO. Lo, sir, here it is.

He gives it to CALISTO.

SEMPRONIO, *aside to* PARMENO. How fast it goes down! Look, if he do not swallow it whole that he may the sooner have done!

CALISTO. It hath done me good. My sons both, farewell. Go look after the old woman and wait for good news. I will reward your labour.

Exit CALISTO.

PARMENO. The devil and ill fortune follow thee!

CELESTINA's *house*

CELESTINA

CELESTINA, *calling to* SEMPRONIO *and* PARMENO, *who are outside.* Come, amorous youths, come, my pearls of gold! It is time for dinner! You are both welcome.

SEMPRONIO, *to* PARMENO. I wonder what devil taught her all her knaveries.

PARMENO. I will tell you: necessity, poverty, and hunger, than which there are no better tutors in the world.

They enter.

CELESTINA, *calling to* ELICIA *and* AREUSA, *who are upstairs.* Hola, wenches, girls, where be you, you fools? Come down, I say, for here are a couple of gallants who would ravish me!

Enter ELICIA *and* AREUSA.

ELICIA, *to* CELESTINA. You have made my cousin wait three hours, but this same lazy-gut Sempronio was the cause, I warrant you, for all this stay. He has no eyes to look upon me.

SEMPRONIO. He who serves another, sweetheart, is not his own man. Be not angry. Let us sit, and fall to.

ELICIA. You are ready at all times to eat!

SEMPRONIO. Come, we will brawl after dinner. Now let us fall to. Mother Celestina, will it please you to sit first?

CELESTINA. No, first sit you down, my son; here is enough for all. Let everyone take their place as they like and sit next her whom he loves best. As for me, I will sit by this jar of wine and this good goblet, for I can live no longer than while I sit with one of these two. In a cold winter's night you cannot have a better warming pan, for when I toss off two of these little pots, why, I feel not a jot of cold all the night long. With this I fur all my clothes at Christmas. This warms my blood. This makes me look ruddy as a rose. This

drives away sorrow better than gold or coral. It adds colour
to the discoloured, courage to the coward, diligence to the
slothful. It comforts the brain. It expels cold from the
stomach. It takes away the stinkingness of the breath. It
makes cold constitutions to be potent. It remedies rheums,
and cures the toothache. It has but this one fault: it lightens
the purse.

SEMPRONIO. Let us eat and talk, aunt, talk and eat, for else
we shall not afterward have time to discourse of the love of
our lost master and Melibea, lovely, gentle Melibea!

ELICIA. And is Melibea so lovely, is she so gentle as you make
her to be? I think my penny to be as good silver as hers!

AREUSA. O sister, hadst thou seen her as I have seen her! All
year long she is mewed up at home where she is daubed
over with a thousand sluttish slibber-slabbers—all which she
must endure for once in a twelvemonth going abroad to be
seen. She anoints her face with honey, parched grapes, and
crushed figs. It is their riches that make such creatures to
be accounted fair, for she has such breasts, being a maid,
as if she had been the mother of three children: they are
for all the world like two great melons. Her belly I have
not seen, but, judging by the rest, I believe it to be as slack
and flaggy as a woman of fifty. I know not what Calisto
should see in her that he should forsake the love of others
whom he may with great ease obtain and far more pleasure
enjoy!

SEMPRONIO. It seems to me, sister, that every pedlar praiseth
his own wares. Quite the contrary is spoken of her throughout the city.

AREUSA. Nothing is farther from the truth than the opinion of
the vulgar. What the vulgar think is vanity! What they
speak is falsehood!

SEMPRONIO. It is no marvel if Calisto love Melibea: he is
noble, she honourably born.

AREUSA. Noble actions make men noble! Let no man search
for virtue in the nobleness of his ancestors!

CELESTINA. Children, as you love me, cease this contentious
talk, and you, Elicia, come to the table again, and sit down!

AREUSA. Let him go hang, sister. Sit down—unless you will have me likewise rise from the table!

ELICIA, *sitting*. I would please *thee* in all things, sister.

SEMPRONIO *laughs*.

Now the evil canker consume thee!

CELESTINA. Son, no more, I pray thee. Tell me, how does Calisto? How fell it out that both of you could slip away from him?

PARMENO. He flung from us, fretting and fuming like a madman, his eyes sparkling fire, his mouth venting curses, and now he is gone to St. Mary Magdalen's, vowing never to come home till he hear that you are come with Melibea in your lap. Your mantle and kirtle and my jerkin are cocksure. For the rest, when he will give it to you, I know not.

CELESTINA. Let it come when it will come! Everything makes the heart merry that is gotten without labour, especially coming from where it leaves so small a gap—from a man of that wealth who with the very scraps of his house would make me of a beggar to become rich! Such as he feel it not, they neither see nor hear, being scorched in the fiery flames of love.

SEMPRONIO. Mother, you and I are of a mind. For here is she present who caused me to become another Calisto, desperate in my doings, leaping over walls, putting my life in danger —which I count time well spent since it gained me so fair a jewel!

ELICIA. I assure thee, thy back is no sooner turned but another is with me whom I love better! And he is a properer man than thou and will not anger me as thou dost!

CELESTINA. Son, all this stir is because you commended Melibea. Go to, my masters, enjoy the flower of fresh and lively youth.

> He that will not when he may
> When he would he shall have nay.

I myself repent me of those hours which I lost when I was young and men did love me. For now I am a decayed creature, withered and full of wrinkles, and nobody will look at me. Yet my mind is still the same: I want rather ability than desire. Fall to your flap, my masters, kiss and clip. As for me I have nothing else to do but to look on and please mine eye. It is some comfort to me yet to be a spectator of your sports. Never stand upon nice terms, for, whilst you sit at board, it is lawful to do anything from the girdle upwards. When you are by yourselves, close together at it in a corner, I will not clap a fine on your heads. The king doth not impose any such taxation; and as for these wenches, they will never accuse you of ravishment. God bless you, but it rejoiceth my heart to see you play thus, you rascals! Watch that you overturn not the table there!

A knock at the door.

CELESTINA. Look who it is, daughter.

ELICIA. Either the voice deceives me, or it is my cousin Lucrecia.

CELESTINA. Let her come in, for she understands somewhat of the matter whereof we discoursed, though, being shut up so close at home, she is hindered in the fruition of her friculation and cannot enjoy her youth as others do.

Enter LUCRECIA.

LUCRECIA. Much good to you, aunt, and to all this great meeting.

CELESTINA. So great, daughter? It appears that you have not known me in my prosperity, which is now some twenty years since. He that sees me now, I wonder his heart doth not burst with sorrow. I tell thee, wench, I have seen at this table nine gallant young wenches at a time! Your noblemen old and young, your churchmen of every station from bishop to sexton, were all at my service, and when I came to a church, my foot was no sooner in but I had as many bonnets vailed to me as a duchess. Spying me half a league off, a priest would drop his prayers and ask how did his wench? 'Twas there they would resolve when they should come to my house.

SEMPRONIO. You make my hair stand on end! Would churchmen fall so low?

CELESTINA. Some were very chaste, others took it upon them to maintain me in my profession. This one sends me in partridges, that one a custard, some other a good suckling pig. Poorer priests brought me the offerings from their altars. And now those days are past! I have eaten all my white bread, and know not how to live!

AREUSA. Do not weep, mother. We are come hither to be merry.

CELESTINA. When I call to mind the merry life which then I led, I have cause to weep. I had the world at will, being served, honoured, and sought after of all.

SEMPRONIO. The remembrance of the good time we have had doth profit us nothing. Mother, we will go aloft and solace ourselves, whilst you give this maid her answer.

Only CELESTINA *and* LUCRECIA *remain.*

CELESTINA. What is the cause, daughter Lucrecia, of your happy coming hither?

LUCRECIA. Believe me, I had almost forgot, with thinking of the merry time you talked of! Mistress, I am sent unto you for my lady's girdle. And my lady entreats you to visit her, and that out of hand for she feels very ill. She is heartsick.

CELESTINA. I marvel that so young a gentlewoman should be pained at the heart.

LUCRECIA, *aside.* The subtle old bawd does her tricks, and then afterwards, when one comes for help, it is news to her forsooth. Traitorous hag, thou knowest well enough what she ails.

CELESTINA. What say you?

LUCRECIA. I say: would we were gone and that you would give me the girdle!

CELESTINA. Let us go. I will carry it along with me.

They start out.

ACT IV

PLEBERIO'S *house*

MELIBEA

MELIBEA, *alone.* O wretch that I am, would it not have been better to have yielded yesterday to Celestina's request and so have contented that gentleman and cured myself than to be thus driven to uncover my heart when haply he will not accept of it, having set his hopes by this on the person of another? And, O my faithful Lucrecia, what wilt *thou* say of me? I know not whether thou hast suspected or no or whether thou art coming even now with that solicitress of my safety. Almighty God, give patience to my wounded heart that I may be able to dissemble my terrible passion! Let not the leaf of my chastity lose its gilding! But how shall I be able to do it? O women, women, why may you not, like men, lay bare your hearts?

LUCRECIA, *outside, to* CELESTINA. Aunt, stay behind this door whilst I go in and see with whom my mistress is talking.
She goes in.

Come in, aunt: she is talking to herself.

MELIBEA. Make fast the door, Lucrecia, and pull down the hanging over it!

CELESTINA, *who has entered.* What is your disease, lady, that you express your torment in maiden blushes?

MELIBEA. Truly, mother, I think there be serpents within that are gnawing on my heart.

CELESTINA, *aside.* It is well! I will be even with you, fool, for your yesterday's anger!

MELIBEA. What's that?

CELESTINA. A great part of health is the desiring of health, but, that I may minister unto you, you must satisfy me in three particulars. First: on which side of your body doth your pain lie most? Second: how long have you had this pain? Third: hath your evil proceeded of any cruel thought which hath taken hold on you? Open the whole truth to your physician as to your confessor.

MELIBEA. My pain is about the heart, its residence near my left pap, but it disperseth itself over every part of my body. Secondly, it hath been so but of late, troubling my sight, changing my countenance, taking away my stomach and my sleep and all my pleasure. Touching the last thing you demanded, I cannot conjecture the cause—neither death of kinsfolk, nor loss of goods, nor any doting dream—save only a kind of alteration caused by your request in the behalf of that gentleman Calisto when you entreated me for the prayer.

CELESTINA. What, madam? Is Calisto so bad a man that but to name him should send forth such poison? Do not believe it. I have another thing in the wind. If your ladyship will give me leave, I will tell you.

MELIBEA. Speak what thou wilt, put thy experience in practice. No remedy is so sharp as my pain. Though it touch mine honour, wrong my reputation, rip and break my flesh, do what thou wilt! If I may find ease, I shall liberally reward thee.

LUCRECIA, *aside.* My mistress has lost her wits. This sorceress hath captivated her will.

CELESTINA, *aside.* A devil is still haunting me: I have escaped Parmeno and fallen upon Lucrecia.

MELIBEA. What is't, mother? What said the wench?

CELESTINA. I cannot tell. But there is not anything more contrary in great cures before stouthearted surgeons than fainting hearts who strike fear into the patient and trouble the surgeon. Therefore, command Lucrecia to be absent.

MELIBEA, *to* LUCRECIA. Get you out! Begone!

LUCRECIA, *aside.* We are all undone.

Exit LUCRECIA.

CELESTINA. Your wound is great and hath need of a sharp

cure. Have patience, for seldom is that cured without pain which in itself is painful: one nail drives out another. Do not conceive hatred, nor give your tongue leave to speak ill of so virtuous a person as Calisto, whom, if you did but know him . . .

MELIBEA. No more of him, for God's sake, you kill me!

CELESTINA. Madam, this is the main point of my cure. There is an invisible needle which you must feel before it come at you and stitch up your wound.

MELIBEA. More pleasing would be it unto me that you would tear my flesh and sinews asunder!

CELESTINA. Without even rending of your garments, your breast was lanced by love. Therefore will I not sunder your flesh to cure the sore.

MELIBEA. How call you this grief?

CELESTINA. Sweet love.

MELIBEA. Tell me, then, what this sweet love may be, for in the very hearing of it named, my heart leaps for joy.

CELESTINA. It is a concealed fire, a pleasing wound, a savoury poison, a sweet hurt, a cheerful torment, and a gentle death.

MELIBEA. According to the contrariety which these names carry, I rest doubtful of my recovery.

CELESTINA. Where God gives a wound, he gives a remedy; as it hurts, so it heals; I know where the flower grows that will free you from this torment.

MELIBEA. How is it called?

CELESTINA. I dare not tell you.

MELIBEA. Speak and spare not.

CELESTINA. Calisto.

MELIBEA *faints*.

If she die in a swoon, they will kill me. Melibea, sweetheart, angel, open your eyes, I say! Lucrecia, run for a jar of water, your lady lies here in a swoon!

MELIBEA, *reviving*. Softly, I pray, do not trouble the house!

CELESTINA. Speak, speak unto me! What will you have me do, my pearl? Whence arose this sudden qualm? I believe my stitches are broken!

MELIBEA. No, it is my honesty that is broken, my bashfulness and shamefulness, which, being my friends, could not absent themselves from my face but they would carry my colour with them, my strength, my speech, my understanding. But now, my faithful secretary, since thou so openly knowest, it is in vain for me to smother it. Thou hast gotten that out of my bosom which I never thought to have uncovered. It is in thy power to do with me what thou wilt.

CELESTINA. Since, madam, you have graced me with so great a confidence, put the managing of this matter into my hands, and you and Calisto shall shortly accomplish your desires.

MELIBEA. Mother and mistress, if thou desirest I should live, so handle the business that I may presently see him.

CELESTINA. See him? You shall both see him and speak with him.

MELIBEA. Speak with him? It is impossible.

CELESTINA. Nothing is impossible to a willing mind.

MELIBEA. Tell me how.

CELESTINA. Marry, within the doors of your house.

MELIBEA. When?

CELESTINA. This night!

MELIBEA. Thou shalt be glorious in mine eyes if thou compass this. But soft: at what hour?

CELESTINA. When the clock strikes twelve.

MELIBEA. Go, begone, my faithful friend, talk with that gentleman and will him to come softly at his appointed hour.

CELESTINA. Your mother is making hitherward already. Farewell.

Exit CELESTINA.

MELIBEA, *to* LUCRECIA, *who has re-entered during the foregoing.* Friend Lucrecia, thou hast seen that I have no power over myself: love hath made me prisoner to this gentleman. I entreat thee to sign what you have seen with the seal of secrecy that I may come to the enjoying of so sweet a love.

LUCRECIA. Since your ladyship hath no other remedy but

either to die or to live, it is meet that you should make choice of the best.

ALISA, *outside, to* CELESTINA. How now, neighbour, what's the matter that you are here thus day by day?

CELESTINA. The thread I sold yesterday lacked a little in weight, and I am come to make it up. God be with you!

ALISA. And with you.

She goes in.

What would this old woman have, daughter?

MELIBEA. She would have sold me a little sublimated mercury.

ALISA. Ay marry, I rather believe this than that which the old lewd hag told me. She was afraid I would have been angry with her, and so she popped me in the mouth with a lie. Take heed of her, daughter: she is an old fox and as false as the devil.

LUCRECIA, *aside.* My old lady's counsel comes too late.

ALISA. I charge you, daughter, if she come hither any more, give her no manner of welcome. Stand upon your honesty and reputation. Be short with her in your answers, and she will never come at you again, for true virtue is more feared than a sword.

MELIBEA. Believe me, madam, she shall never come at me more.

St. Mary Magdalen's

CELESTINA *outside.* CALISTO, PARMENO, SEMPRONIO *inside*

CELESTINA. O thrice-happy day! O joy! But I see Parmeno and Sempronio going into St. Mary Magdalen's. I will after them and if I meet with Calisto we will all along together to his house to demand the reward.

SEMPRONIO, *to* CALISTO. Take heed, sir, lest by your long stay you give occasion of talk, for it is commonly spoken amongst the people that he is an hypocrite that is too devout. Uncover not your grief unto strangers since the drum is in their hands who know best how to beat it, and your business is in her hands who knows best how to manage it.

CALISTO. Whose hands?

SEMPRONIO. Celestina's.

CELESTINA, *inside.* Who names Celestina? What sayest thou of this slave of Calisto's?

CALISTO. Thou joy of the world, ease of my passions, relieveress of my pain, speak!

CELESTINA. Sir, let us first go more privately, and, as we walk to your house, I will tell you that which shall make you glad.

PARMENO, *to* SEMPRONIO. The old woman looks merrily.

SEMPRONIO. Soft, listen what she says.

They leave the church.

CELESTINA. All this day, sir, have I been labouring in your business and have neglected other affairs which did much concern me. But all is well lost since I have brought your business to so good an end: Melibea is wholly at your service.

CALISTO. What do I hear?

CELESTINA. Nay, she is more at your service than at that of her father Pleberio.

CALISTO. Melibea—my mistress? I am *her* servant, I am her slave! She is all my desire, she is my life!

SEMPRONIO. Good sir, you cut off Celestina in the midst of her discourse. It were better you should give her something for her pains.

CALISTO. Well spoken! Mother, instead of a mantle and kirtle, take this little chain, put it about your neck—and go on with your discourse and my joy!

PARMENO, *aside, to* SEMPRONIO. *Little* chain? Heard you him, Sempronio? I will not give my part thereof for half a mark of gold.

SEMPRONIO. Thou hast two ears and but one tongue: as thou lov'st me, brother, hear and hold your peace.

CELESTINA. Melibea loves you and desires to see you.

CALISTO. You my servants, am I here? Look whether I am awake or not! O God, I beseech Thee this may not prove a dream! Tell me, mother, dost thou make sport with me?

CELESTINA. Whether I jest or no, yourself shall see by going this night to her house as the clock strikes twelve, that you may talk together through the chinks of the door. From her own mouth you shall know my solicitude and her desire.

CALISTO. Can so great a blessing light upon Calisto? No! I am not capable of so great a glory!

CELESTINA. I have heard that it is harder to suffer prosperous than adverse fortune, but it is strange, sir, that you will not consider the time that you have spent in her service, nor the person whom you have made to be your means. Celestina is on your side: for you I would make mountains of craggy rocks to grow plain and smooth.

CALISTO. Did you not tell me that she would come to me of her own accord?

CELESTINA. Upon her very knees.

SEMPRONIO. I fear me it is a trap to catch us all. So men use crooked pins wrapped in bread, poisonous pills rolled in sugar.

PARMENO. The songs of the sirens deceive the simple mariner. Even so with her sudden concession of love she will seize on a whole drove of us and purge her innocency with Calisto's honour and our deaths.

CALISTO. Peace, you suspicious rascals, will you make me believe that angels can do ill?

SEMPRONIO. What, will you still play the heretic?

Aside, to PARMENO.

If the play prove foul, he shall pay for all: we will take to our heels.

CELESTINA. Sir, you are in the right, and these in the wrong. And so I leave you to your joys. If you have further occasion to use me, you shall find me ready.

PARMENO *laughs.*

SEMPRONIO. Why dost thou laugh?

PARMENO. To see what haste the old trot makes. She thinks every hour a year till she be clear away with the chain.

SEMPRONIO. What would you have an old bawd do (that useth to patch up seven virginities at a clap for two pieces of silver) but make it safe and sure for fear lest he should take it from her again after he hath had his desire? But let us take heed when we come to divide the spoil.

CALISTO. Mother, fare you well, I will lay me down to sleep awhile to redeem the nights past and prepare the better for the night to come.

PLEBERIO'S *house*

CALISTO, SEMPRONIO, PARMENO

CALISTO, *with* PARMENO *and* SEMPRONIO. Now it strikes twelve, a good hour.

PARMENO. We are near unto the place.

CALISTO. Go thou, Parmeno, and peep in at the door, to see if that lady be come or no.

PARMENO. Who? I, sir? She may be moved to anger in seeing so many acquainted with that which she secretly desires.

CALISTO. This is sound advice. I will go myself.

He goes to the door.

SEMPRONIO. Be in readiness upon the first alarm to take to thy heels.

PARMENO. I am glad, brother, thou hast advised me to that which otherwise, for fear of thee, I should never have done.

SEMPRONIO. O my friend, how good it is to live together in love! Though Celestina should prove good to us in no other thing, yet in this hath she done us service.

CALISTO, *at the door.* Mistress, be you there?

LUCRECIA *and* MELIBEA *are on the other side of the door.*

LUCRECIA, *going a little nearer.* Who speaks?

CALISTO. He that comes at your command.

MELIBEA. Go a little aside, Lucrecia. Sir, who willed you to come?

CALISTO. She whom I may not merit to serve.

MELIBEA. You have already received her answer. I know not what more you can get of my life than what I then made known.

CALISTO. Miserable Calisto, how hast thou been mocked! Cozening Celestina, why didst thou falsify this lady's message? Didst thou not say she would be favourable? Miserable that I am, whom shall I trust? In whom shall I find any faith? Where is truth to be had? Where the faithful friend?

MELIBEA. Now cease, good sir, your just complaints. Thou weepest out of grief, judging me cruel; I weep out of joy, seeing thee faithful.

CALISTO. O my heart's joy, what tongue can be sufficient to give thee thanks? I stand amazed!

MELIBEA. My heart hath not one moment been absent from thee. As soon as that woman returned thy sweet name to my remembrance, I appointed our meeting at this place and time. Dispose of my person according to thy pleasure.

CALISTO. These doors debar us of our joy!

MELIBEA. I curse these locks and bars as also mine own weak strength!

CALISTO. O troublesome and sport-hindering doors! Give me leave, sweet lady, to call my servants and break them open!

PARMENO, *to* SEMPRONIO. Hearest thou what he says? We shall run into a peck of troubles!

SEMPRONIO. Peace! She will not consent.

MELIBEA. If you break down these cruel doors, though haply we should not presently be heard, yet tomorrow there would arise a terrible suspicion in my father's house, which, in the turning of a hand, would be noised through the whole city.

SEMPRONIO. We are far enough off. Upon the very first noise, we will take to our heels.

PARMENO. Well spoken! Let us shun death, for we are young, and not to desire to die nor to kill is not cowardice but natural goodness. I stand sideling, my legs apart, my left foot foremost, the skirts of my cassock tucked under my girdle, my buckler close to my arm. I believe I should outrun the swiftest buck.

SEMPRONIO. I have bound my sword and buckler together that they may not fall when I run. Hark! Hearest, thou, Parmeno? Away! Begone! Make toward Celestina's house that we may not be cut off on our way to our own!

They run.

PARMENO. Fly, fly, you run too slowly! Throw away thy buckler and all.

SEMPRONIO. Have they killed our master?

PARMENO. I know not. Say nothing to me. Run and hold your peace! He is the least of my care.

SEMPRONIO. Parmeno! Turn and be still! It is nothing but the watch!

PARMENO, *stopping.* They have not left me one drop of blood in my body. Never was I in the like fear.

SEMPRONIO. Turn back, for it is the watch, that's certain.

They turn back.

MELIBEA, *to* CALISTO. What noise is that?

CALISTO. It should be my men who disarm as many as pass by.

MELIBEA. Are they many that you brought?

CALISTO. No more than two, but should half a dozen set upon them, they would not be long in disarming them, they are such true and approved metal. Were it not for thy honour, they would have broken these doors in pieces and, had we been heard, have freed thyself and me from thy father's servants.

PARMENO, *to* CALISTO. Sist, sist, hear you, sir? Begone, for here is a great company with torches. Unless you make haste you will be seen and known.

CALISTO. Believe me, lady, the fear of death would not work so much upon me as the fear of thy honour doth. I take my leave. My next coming, as thou hast ordered it, shall be by the garden.

MELIBEA. Be it so. And happiness go with thee.

PLEBERIO *and* ALISA, *in another room.*

PLEBERIO. Wife, are you asleep?

ALISA. No, sir.

PLEBERIO. Do not you hear some noise in your daughter's chamber?

ALISA. Marry do I. Melibea!

PLEBERIO. I will call louder. Melibea!

MELIBEA. Sir?

PLEBERIO. Who stirs?

MELIBEA. Lucrecia, sir, who went forth to fetch some water.

PLEBERIO. Sleep again, daughter, I thought it had been something else.

LUCRECIA, *to* MELIBEA. A little noise can wake them. Methought they spoke fearfully.

CALISTO's *house*

CALISTO, SEMPRONIO, PARMENO

CALISTO. Tell me, Parmeno, what dost thou think of the old woman whom thou didst dispraise? What could we have done without her?

PARMENO. I advised you as I thought best, but now I see Celestina is changed from what she was.

CALISTO. Didst thou hear what passed between me and my mistress? What did you do all that while? Were you not afraid?

SEMPRONIO. Of what? All the world could not make us afraid!

CALISTO. Took you not a little nap?

SEMPRONIO. I did not so much as sit down but watched as diligently as a cat for a mouse. And Parmeno, he was as glad when he spied the torches coming as a wolf when he spies a flock of sheep.

CALISTO. It is natural in him to be valiant: the fox, though he may change his hair, cannot change his nature. My sons, I am much bound unto you; pray to heaven for success, and doubt not but I will reward your service. Good night.

Exit CALISTO.

PARMENO. Shall we go sleep, Sempronio? Or break our fast?

SEMPRONIO. Ere it be day I will get me to Celestina's house and see if I can recover my part in the chain. She is crafty and I will not give her time to invent some trick and cozen us of our shares.

PARMENO. Let us go together, and, if she stand upon points, let us put her into such a fear that she will betray herself. For money goes beyond all friendship.

They go.

CELESTINA'S *house*

CELESTINA, SEMPRONIO, PARMENO

SEMPRONIO, *outside, to* PARMENO. Her bed is hard by this little window.

He knocks.

CELESTINA, *inside.* Who knocks?

SEMPRONIO. Celestina, open the door, your sons be here.

CELESTINA. I have no sons that be abroad at this time of night.

SEMPRONIO. It is Parmeno and Sempronio.

CELESTINA. Ye mad lads, you wanton wags, enter, enter!

They enter.

How chance you come so early? It is but break of day. How goes the world? Calisto's hopes, are they alive or dead? How stands it with him?

SEMPRONIO. How, mother? Had it not been for us, his soul ere this had gone seeking its eternal rest.

CELESTINA. Have you been in such danger? How was it, I pray?

PARMENO. Provide something for his and my breakfast. When we have eaten, our choler will be somewhat allayed.

CELESTINA. The pox canker my carcass to death, but thou lookest so fierce and ghastly! Sempronio, what hath befallen you?

SEMPRONIO. Mother, I have brought hither my arms all broken and battered, my sword like a saw, my casque dented in with blows. My master shall this night have access to his mistress' garden, but to furnish myself anew I know not where to have one penny.

CELESTINA. Go to your master for it!

SEMPRONIO. He for his part hath done enough. He hath given us a hundred crowns in gold. He hath given us a chain.

CELESTINA. Art thou well in thy wits, Sempronio? What has thy remuneration to do with my reward? As soon as I came home, I gave the chain to this fool Elicia that she might look upon it. She for her life cannot call to mind what she hath done with it, and all this livelong night neither she nor I have slept a wink for grief thereof. At the time that we missed it came in some friends of mine, and I am afraid lest they have taken it away with them. But now, my sons, that I may speak home to the point: if your master gave me anything, what he gave me is mine. I have twice endangered my life for it. More blades have I blunted in his service than you both. More hose and shoes have I worn out. And, my sons, all this costs me good money, besides my skill which I got not warming my tail over the fire. I get *my* living by trade and travail; you yours with recreation and delight; and therefore are you not to expect equal recompense. But because I will deal kindly with you, if my chain be found, I will give each of you a pair of scarlet breeches, which is the comeliest habit that young men can wear. If this will not content you, to your own harm be it!

SEMPRONIO. How doth penury increase with plenty! How often did this old woman say that I should have all the profit that should grow from this business!

PARMENO. Let her give thee that which she promised or let us take it from her!

CELESTINA. I perceive on which foot you halt. Because you think I will make you captives to Elicia and Areusa and provide you no fresh ware, you quarrel thus with me for money! Be still, my boys, she who could help you with these will not stick to furnish you with half a score of handsome wenches apiece!

SEMPRONIO. You talk of chalk and we of cheese. Lay aside these tricks, and give us two parts of that which you received of Calisto. We know you too well.

CELESTINA. I am an old woman of God's making, no worse than other women are. I live by my occupation as other women do. For the life I lead, whether it be good or bad, heaven knows my heart. And do not think to misuse me, for there is justice for all. And you, Parmeno, do not think that I am thy slave because thou knowest my life past and all that passed betwixt me and that unfortunate mother of thine, for she also was wont to use me on this fashion when she was disposed to play her pranks.

PARMENO. Do not hit me in the teeth with memorials of my mother unless thou meanest I should send thee unto her!

CELESTINA. Elicia, Elicia, come down quickly and bring my mantle! I will hie me to the Justice and there rail at you like a madwoman! What do you mean, to menace me in my own house, an old woman of sixty years of age? Go and wreak your anger upon men!

SEMPRONIO. Thou covetous old crib that art ready to die with the thirst of gold, cannot a third part of the gain content thee?

CELESTINA. Out of my house in the devil's name, you and your companion with you! A pox on you both!

SEMPRONIO. Cry, bawl, make a noise, we care not. Either look to perform your promise or end your days.

ELICIA, *who has come downstairs.* Hold him, Parmeno, for fear the fool *should* kill her in his madness!

CELESTINA. Justice! Neighbours, help! Murder! Here be ruffians that will murder me!

SEMPRONIO. Ruffians, you whore? Ruffians, you bawd? Sorceress! Witch! I shall send thee post to hell!

He stabs her.

CELESTINA. Ay me, I am slain. Confession, confession!

PARMENO. Be brief with her, lest the neighbours chance to hear! Kill her, kill her!

CELESTINA *moans and dies.*

ELICIA. My mother is dead, and with her my happiness. The extremity of justice fall upon you!

SEMPRONIO. Fly, fly, Parmeno, the people begin to flock hither. See, see, yonder comes the watch!

PARMENO. There is no means of escape. They have made good the door.

SEMPRONIO. Let us leap out at these windows and die rather than fall into the hands of justice.

PARMENO. Leap then! I will follow.

They leap through a high window.

CALISTO's *house*

CALISTO

CALISTO. O how daintily have I slept! Contentment and quietude have proceeded from my joy. What happiness do I now possess! O my sweet lady and dearest love, what dost thou think on now? Thinkst thou on me, Melibea, or somebody else? O most fortunate Calisto, if only it be true and no dream! Now I remember, my two servants waited on me: if they shall affirm it be no dream I am bound to believe it. Tristan!

Enter TRISTAN.

TRISTAN. Sir?

CALISTO. Call hither Sempronio and Parmeno.

TRISTAN. I shall, sir.

Exit TRISTAN.

CALISTO, *singing*.

> Now sleep and take thy rest,
> Once griev'd and painèd wight,
> Since she now loves thee best
> Who is thy heart's delight.
> Let joy be thy soul's guest
> And care be banished quite
> Since she hath thee exprest
> To be her favourite.

TRISTAN, *returning*. There is not so much as a boy in the house.

CALISTO. Open the windows and see whether it be day.

TRISTAN. Sir, it is broad day.

CALISTO. Go again, and see if thou canst find them; and wake me not till it be dinner time.

TRISTAN, *going*. I will go down and stand at the door that my master may take out his full sleep. But what outcry do I hear in the market place? Yonder comes Sosia, my master's footboy: he will tell me. Look how the rogue comes pulling and tearing of his hair! What's the matter, Sosia?

Enter SOSIA.

SOSIA. Misfortune! Dishonour! O unhappy young men!

TRISTAN. What's the matter?

SOSIA. Sempronio and Parmeno!

TRISTAN. What of them?

SOSIA. They lie slain in the street!

TRISTAN. Is it true? Let us haste with these tidings to our master!

They go to CALISTO's *room*.

SOSIA. Master! Master!

CALISTO. Did I not will you I should not be wakened?

SOSIA. Sempronio and Parmeno lie beheaded in the market place as public malefactors!

CALISTO. Heaven help me! But I know not whether I may believe this news. Didst thou see them?

SOSIA. I saw them, sir.

CALISTO. Take heed what thou sayest, for this night they were with me.

SOSIA. But rose too early to their deaths.

CALISTO. My loyal servants! My chiefest followers! For pity's sake, Sosia, what was the cause of their deaths?

SOSIA. The cause, sir, was published by the common hangman who delivered with a loud voice: "Justice hath commanded that these murderers be put to death."

CALISTO. Who was it they slew? Who might it be? It is not four hours since they left me. What was he for a man?

SOSIA. It was a woman, sir, one whom they call Celestina.

CALISTO. What's that?

SOSIA. That which you heard me tell you, sir.

CALISTO. If this be true, kill thou me too. For sure there is more ill behind if that Celestina be slain, that hath the slash over her face.

SOSIA. It is the very same, sir, for I saw her stretched out in her own house, and her maid weeping by her, having received in her body above thirty several wounds.

CALISTO. Spake they unto thee?

SOSIA. That they might not fall into the hands of the watch, they leapt out of a high window. One had his brains beaten out. The other had both his arms broken and his face so sorely bruised that it was all of a gore-blood. When their heads were chopped off, I think, they scarce felt what harm was done them.

CALISTO. O mine honour, my reputation, how dost thou go from table to table, from mouth to mouth! O my secret actions, how openly will you walk through every street! Tell me, Sosia, what was the cause they killed her?

SOSIA. The maid who sat weeping over her made known the cause to as many as would hear it, saying that they slew her because she would not let them share in that chain of gold which you had lately given her.

CALISTO. O Fortune, how hast thou beaten me! And yet by adversities the heart is proved, whether it be of oak or elder. Come what will come, I will accomplish her desire for whose sake all this hath happened. For it is better to pursue the glory which I expect than the loss of those that are dead; they would have been slain at some other time, if not now. And the old woman was wicked and false; this was a judgment of God upon her. Sosia and Tristan shall accompany me, and carry ladders, for the walls are high.

PLEBERIO's *garden*

MELIBEA, LUCRECIA, SOSIA, TRISTAN, CALISTO

MELIBEA. The gentleman stays long. Tell me, Lucrecia, will he come or no?

LUCRECIA. I conceive, madam, he hath some just cause of stay.

MELIBEA. I am afraid lest some misfortune may befall him as he is on his way. Hark! What steps are those?

SOSIA, *on the other side of the wall.* Set the ladder here, Tristan.

CALISTO. I will in alone, for I hear my mistress.

CALISTO *climbs into the garden.*

MELIBEA. Take heed, my dear lord, how you leap, I shall swoon in seeing it. Take more leisure in coming down the ladder!

CALISTO. My lady and my glory! I embrace and hug thee in mine arms! A turbation of pleasure seizeth on my person!

MELIBEA. My lord, rejoice in that wherein I rejoice: which is to view and touch thee. But do not ask that which, being taken away, is not in thy power to restore.

CALISTO. Dear lady, it is not in any man that is a man to forbear in such a case; much less in me, having swum through this sea of thy desire and mine own. After so many travails, will you deny me entrance to the sweet haven where I may find some ease of all my sorrows?

MELIBEA. Content yourself in the enjoying of this outwardness!

Do not rob me of the greatest jewel which nature hath enriched me with!

CALISTO. Madam, what mean you? Pardon, sweet lady, these my impudent hands if too presumptuously they press upon you! Though once they never thought to touch thy garments, they now have leave to lay themselves with gentle palm on thy dainty body, this white, soft, delicate flesh.

MELIBEA. Lucrecia, go aside a little.

CALISTO. And why, madam? I should be proud to have such witnesses of my glory.

MELIBEA. So would not I, when I do amiss.

LUCRECIA *goes aside.*

Passage of time.

SOSIA, *on the other side of the wall.* Tristan, thou hear'st how the gear goes?

TRISTAN. I hold my master the happiest man that lives and, though I am but a boy, methinks I could give as good an account of such a business as my master!

SOSIA. To such a jewel who would not reach out his hand? And he hath paid well for it: a couple of his servants served to make sauce for this his love.

MELIBEA. O my lord, how couldst thou find in thy heart that I should lose the name and crown of a virgin for so momentary a pleasure? O my poor mother, if thou knewest this, how cruel a butcher of thyself and me wouldst thou become! O my honoured father, how have I wronged thy reputation and given place to the undoing of thy house! Traitor to myself, why did I not foresee the error which would ensue by thy entrance, Calisto?

SOSIA, *as before.* What's done cannot be undone. You should have sung this song before.

The clock strikes three.

CALISTO. Methinks we have not been here above an hour, and now the clock strikes three.

MELIBEA. My lord, for God's love, now that I am thy mistress, deny me not thy sight. And let thy coming be ever at this secret place and at the selfsame hour. Farewell, my lord. Thou wilt not be seen, for it is dark, nor I heard, for it is not yet day.

CALISTO *goes to the wall.*

CALISTO. Bring hither the ladder.

SOSIA. Sir, it is ready.

CALISTO *descends.*

ACT V

Several weeks later. CALISTO'S *house*

SOSIA, TRISTAN

SOSIA. What thinkest thou of Calisto?

TRISTAN. On the one side he is oppressed with sadness for Sempronio and Parmeno, and on the other side transported with the gladsome delight which he hath enjoyed these nights with his Melibea. And where two such strong and contrary passions meet, thou knowest with what violence they will work upon a feeble subject.

SOSIA. Dost thou think he feels grief for those that are dead? If she did not grieve more whom I see here out of the window go along the street, she would not wear a veil of such a colour.

TRISTAN. Who is that, brother?

SOSIA. Seest thou that mournful maid which wipes the tears from her eyes? That is Elicia, Celestina's servant and Sempronio's friend, and in the house you see her entering there dwells a lovely woman. She is half-courtesan, yet happy is he that can win her. Her name is Areusa, for whose sake poor Parmeno endured many a miserable night. And she, poor soul, is nothing pleased with his death.

AREUSA's *house*

AREUSA, ELICIA

AREUSA. O my Parmeno, how doth thy death torment me!

ELICIA. Great sorrow, great loss! That which I show is but little to that which I feel! My heart is blacker than my mantle, my bowels than my veil!

She breaks down, sobbing.

AREUSA. But, being that this ill-success hath ensued and, being that their lives cannot be restored by tears, do not, sister, vex thyself in weeping out thine eyes. I grieve as much, and yet thou seest with what patience I pass it over.

ELICIA. Wretch that I am, I am ready to run out of my wits! Whither shall I go? I have lost money, meat, drink, and clothes! I have lost my friend! And that which grieves me most is to see that this villain Calisto, who hath no sense nor feeling of his servants' death, goes every night to visit his filth Melibea, feasting and solacing himself in her company, whilst she grows proud, glorying to see so much blood sacrificed for her!

AREUSA. If this be so, of whom can we revenge ourselves better? He that hath eaten the meat, let him pay for it . . . There is a ruffian, one Centurio, who even now went from me sad and heavy, for that I would not impose any service upon him. If this villain prove not a worse executioner for Calisto than Sempronio was for Celestina, never trust me more. Now tell me, cousin, how this business goes.

ELICIA. Sosia, Calisto's groom, accompanies him . . .

AREUSA. Enough! Send hither this Sosia. I will take him in hand.

Passage of time.

A knock on the door.

Who is't that knocks?

SOSIA, *outside.* Sosia.

AREUSA, *to* ELICIA. Hide yourself, sister, behind these hangings, and thou shalt see how I will puff him up.

Enter SOSIA.

My Sosia! My inward friend—whom I have longed to know —though perhaps he knew it not! I will hug thee in mine arms, for I see report comes short and there are more virtues in thee than I have been told of. How thou dost resemble my unfortunate Parmeno! Tell me, gentle sir, did you ever know me before?

SOSIA. The fame, gentlewoman, of your graces flies with so swift a wing that you need not marvel if you be of more known than knowing.

ELICIA, *aside.* To see how the silly fellow exceeds himself! He that hath seen him go to water his horses, riding without a saddle, with his naked legs hanging down beneath his canvas frock, and should now see him, thus handsome and well-suited, why, he would crow like a cockerel!

AREUSA. False and deceitful praises are common among men but, Sosia, that thereby thou shouldst think to gain my love is needless, for thou hast gained it already. There are two things, Sosia, which caused me to send unto thee. What they are I will leave to thyself to relate.

SOSIA. Answer for me your own questions: I shall confirm whatever you propound.

AREUSA. First, then, did I send for thee that I might give thee to understand how much I love thee; secondly, that I may admonish thee not to tell thy secrets to any, for thou seest what befell Parmeno and Sempronio. There came one unto me and said thou hadst told him of the love betwixt Calisto and Melibea and how thou goest along with Calisto night by night. Take heed, sir, and do not think thy friend will keep thy secret when thyself cannot keep it. When thou goest to that lady's house, make no noise, for some have told me that thou canst not contain thyself.

SOSIA. O what busybodies be they who abuse your ears with such tales! And some others, perhaps, because they see me go a-nights, when the moon shines, to water my horses, whistling and singing, conceive an evil suspicion, and of this suspicion make certainties. Nor is Calisto so foolish that he should go about such a business but that he will first be sure that all is quiet. And less are you to suppose that he goeth every night unto her: such a duty will not endure a daily visitation!

AREUSA. If you love me then, my dear, that I may accuse these busybodies to their faces, acquaint me with the days you determine to go thither.

SOSIA. Mistress, this very night, when the clock shall strike twelve, they have appointed to meet in the garden.

AREUSA. On which side of the garden, my sweetheart—that I may contradict these babblers?

SOSIA. By the street where the fat hostess dwells, just on the back side of her house.

AREUSA. Brother Sosia, this shall suffice, and so a good speed of thee, for I have other business to despatch.

SOSIA. Courteous sweet mistress, your own best wishes attend you.

Exit SOSIA. ELICIA *comes out.*

AREUSA. Now that we have squeezed this orange, I think it not amiss to call hither that dog's face Centurio.

Passage of time.

Enter CENTURIO.

CENTURIO. Command me, mistress, in such things as I know: to kill this or that man; to cut off a leg or an arm; to slash any woman over the face that shall stand in competition with thee. Such trifles shall be no sooner said than done.

AREUSA. I take you at your word. Revenge me upon a gentleman called Calisto, who hath wronged me and my cousin.

CENTURIO. Incontinently! But hath he received confession?

AREUSA. His soul is no charge of thine.

CENTURIO. Then let us send him to dine in hell without confession!

AREUSA. Fail me not, I advise you. This night, if you will, you may take him napping.

CENTURIO. No more! I apprehend your meaning! But tell me, how many accompany him?

AREUSA. Only two, and those, young fellows.

CENTURIO. This is too poor a pittance. My sword will have but a short supper: it would fare better at some other time.

AREUSA. I must not be fed with delays: I would see whether sayings and doings eat together at your table.

CENTURIO. If my sword should tell you the deeds it hath done it would want time to utter them. What peoples church-yards but my sword? Who makes surgeons rich but my sword? Who slices the helmets of Calatayud? Who shreds the casks of Almazan? For this blade the name of Centurio was given to my grandfather!

AREUSA. We would not have to do with your pedigree. Re-solve suddenly if you will do that I spake to you of.

CENTURIO. Make your own choice what death you will have him die! For I can show you a bead-roll wherein are set down some seven hundred and seventy sorts of deaths, which, when you have seen, you may choose that which likes you best.

ELICIA. He is too bloody for this business, Areusa!

AREUSA. Sister, hold your peace.

CENTURIO. Some I use like sieves, pricking them full of holes with my poniard! Some I cut in a large size, giving them a mortal wound, a fearful *stoccado!* And now and then I use my cudgel or *bastinado* that my sword may keep holiday!

ELICIA. Bastinado him, I pray you, for I would have him beaten but not slain!

AREUSA. Sister, let Melibea weep as you have done. Centurio, so long as you revenge us on him, any way shall content us.

CENTURIO. Unless he take to his heels, he is going to hell, I warrant you! I will give him his passport!

AREUSA. God direct thy hand! And so, farewell.

CENTURIO *goes outside.*

CENTURIO. Now, O headstrong whores, will I think how I may excuse myself of my promise, and in such sort, too, that they may be persuaded that I used all possible diligence to ex-ecute their desire. I will feign myself sick. But then they will be at me again when I am well. I will say I have forced this Calisto to fly. But then they will ask who was with him and by what marks I knew them. And so the fat is in the fire. What counsel shall I take that may comply with mine own safety and their desire? I will send for lame Thraso and his companions, and tell them to go and make a clattering with their swords and bucklers in manner of a fray. This is a sure course and no other hurt can follow save to make this Calisto get him home to bed.

PLEBERIO's *garden*

CALISTO, SOSIA, TRISTAN, LUCRECIA, MELIBEA

CALISTO, *outside, to* SOSIA *and* TRISTAN. Set up the ladder, and see you make no noise, for I hear my mistress' tongue. I will get me to the top of the wall, and there stand awhile to see if I can hear any token of her love to me.
He does so.

MELIBEA, *inside the garden.* Sing on, Lucrecia, sing on, till my lord come, and let us go aside into this green walk that they that pass by may not hear.

LUCRECIA.

> Sweet is the fount, the place,
> I drank at, being dry;
> More sweet Calisto's face
> In Melibea's eye.
> And though that it be night,
> His sight my heart will cheer,
> And when he down shall light
> O how I'll clip my dear!
> The wolf for joy doth leap
> To see the lambkins move,
> The kid joys in the teat
> And thou joy'st in thy love.
> Never was loving wight
> Of's friend desirèd so;
> Ne'er walks of more delight
> Nor nights more free from woe.

MELIBEA. Methinks I see that which thou singest. It is as if
he stood before me. Go on: I will bear a part with thee.

LUCRECIA *and* MELIBEA.

> Sweet trees who shade this mould
> Of earth, your heads down bend
> When you those eyes behold
> Of my best-lovèd friend.
> Fair stars whose bright appear
> Both beautify the sky,
> Why wake ye not my dear
> If he asleeping lie?

MELIBEA, *alone.*

> You birds whose warblings prove
> Aurora draweth near,
> Go fly and tell my love
> That I expect him here.
> The night doth posting move
> Yet comes he not again.
> God grant some other love
> Do not my love detain!

CALISTO. The sweetness of her voice hath ravished me! Dear
lady and glory of my life, if thou lovest me, give not over
thy singing!

MELIBEA. My desire of thee was that which made me air my
notes; now that thou art come, that desire disappears.

CALISTO. O interrupted melody, short-timed pleasure!

MELIBEA. The whole garden delights in thy coming! Look on
the moon, how bright she shines! Look on the clouds, how
speedily they rack away! Hark to the fountain, how sweet
a murmur! Hark to the cypresses, how one bough makes
peace with another! Behold these silent shades, how dark
they are, for the concealing of our sports!

LUCRECIA *makes as if to embrace* CALISTO.

Lucrecia, art thou mad with pleasure? Touch not my love!

LUCRECIA *withdraws to one side.*

CALISTO. My sweet mistress! My life's happiness!

He takes her in his arms.

MELIBEA. Sir, as thou art the pattern of all courtesy, if thou

wouldst learn if my dress be of silk or wool, why dost thou
lay hands upon my petticoats, which assuredly are of linen?

CALISTO. He, madam, that wisheth to eat the bird first removes
the feathers!

LUCRECIA, *aside.* Here's a life indeed. I feel myself melt like
snow beneath the sun.

MELIBEA. Shall I send Lucrecia to fetch you sweetmeats?

CALISTO. No sweetmeats for me save this thy body! Wish
rather that I should not let slip the least moment in enjoying such a treasure!

LUCRECIA, *aside.* My head aches with hearing, and yet their
lips ache not with kissing. Sure, they will make me gnaw
the finger of my glove to pieces!

A clattering outside.

SOSIA, *outside.* Out you ruffians! Out you rogues!

CALISTO. Madam, that is Sosia's voice, suffer me to see that
they do not kill him, for there is nobody with him but a
little page.

SOSIA. Yea? Are you come again? I shall fleece you, you
rascals!

CALISTO. Lady, if you love me, let me go. The ladder stands
ready.

He leaves her.

MELIBEA. Why dost thou go so furiously and fast to hazard
thy life amongst thou knowest not whom? Lucrecia, come
quickly, for Calisto is gone to thrust himself into a quarrel.

CALISTO *climbs the wall.*

TRISTAN. Stay, sir! They are gone! It is nobody but lame
Thraso and his companions that made a noise as they passed
by. Take heed, sir! Hold fast by the ladder lest you fall!

CALISTO *falls from the top of the wall.*

CALISTO. Our Lady help me! I am dead! Confession!

TRISTAN. Sosia! Our master is fallen from the ladder! He neither
speaks nor wags!

SOSIA, *bending over* CALISTO's *body.* Master! Master! Do you
hear, sir? Let us call a little at this other door. He hears on

neither ear. He is as dead as a doornail. There is no more life in him than in my grandfather who died some hundred years since.

LUCRECIA. Hark, hark, madam, what mischance is this?

TRISTAN. My master, my master is dead! He is fallen headlong down. Dead and without confession! Help, Sosia, help to gather up these brains that lie scattered among the stones! Let us put them back in his head!

MELIBEA. What is this? Help me, Lucrecia, to get up this wall that I may see my sorrow! Is all my joy turned to smoke?

LUCRECIA. What's the matter, Tristan, why dost thou weep so?

TRISTAN. My master Calisto hath fallen from the ladder and is dead. His head is in three pieces. He perished without confession. Bear this sad message to his new mistress that she never more expect him. Sosia, take up his feet and let us carry his body hence that he may not suffer dishonour in this place.

They do so.

MELIBEA. So soon to see my sorrows come upon me!

LUCRECIA. Tear not your face, madam, rend not your hair! Out alas! Arise from the ground! Let not your father find you in so suspicious a place!

MELIBEA. My time is come. I am a dead woman. That I should let thee go! Ungrateful mortals, we never know our happiness until we want it!

LUCRECIA. Let us into your chamber. Lay you down on your bed, and I will call your father. We will feign illness, since to hide this it is impossible.

PLEBERIO's *house*

PLEBERIO, LUCRECIA, *in* PLEBERIO's *room.* MELIBEA *in her own room*

PLEBERIO. What sudden sickness hath seized upon her, that I cannot have the leisure to put on my clothes?

LUCRECIA. I know not, sir. But if you will see her alive, come quickly.

They go to MELIBEA'S *room.*

PLEBERIO. Lift up the hangings, open this window, that I may take a full view of her. Daughter, speak unto me, open thy gladsome eyes!

MELIBEA. Ay me!

PLEBERIO. Thy mother, when she heard thou wast ill, fell into a swoon. Tell me, sweet soul, the cause of thy sorrow.

MELIBEA. Before you can cure it, you must take out my heart, for the malady lies in the most secret place thereof.

PLEBERIO. Youth should be an enemy to care, and a friend to mirth. Rise then, and let us take some fresh air by the riverside. Do not cast thyself away!

MELIBEA. Let us go whither you please, and, if it stand with your liking, to the top of the tower, from whence I may enjoy the sight of the ships that pass to and fro.

PLEBERIO. Let us go, and take Lucrecia with us.

MELIBEA. Father, I pray, cause some musical instrument to be sent unto me. Delightful harmony will mitigate my sorrow.

PLEBERIO. I will go myself and will it to be provided.

Exit PLEBERIO. MELIBEA *and* LUCRECIA *go to the top of the tower.*

MELIBEA. Friend Lucrecia, this place is high. I am loth to lose my father's company. Step down and entreat him to come to the foot of this tower, for I have a word or two to tell him that he should deliver to my mother.

LUCRECIA. I go, madam.

Exit LUCRECIA.

MELIBEA. All have left me, I am now alone. The manner of my death falls pat to my mind; it is some ease unto me that Calisto and I shall meet again so soon. I will make fast the door that nobody may stop me on my journey to him. Things have fallen out luckily. I have time to recount to my father 'leberio the cause of this my short and sudden end. I shall ·ch wrong his silver hairs and shall work great woe unto

him by this my error, leaving him in desolation all the days
of his life; but it is not in my power to do otherwise. Thou,
O God, who art witness of my words, Thou seest the small
power that I have over my passion! My senses are taken
with the love of the deceased gentleman who hath de-
prived me of the love which I bear to my living parents.

PLEBERIO *comes to the foot of the tower.*

PLEBERIO. Daughter Melibea, shall I come up to you?

MELIBEA. No, Father, you shall see the death of your only
daughter. Hear the last words that ever I shall speak. I am
sure you hear the lamentation throughout the city: the ring-
ing of bells, the scriking and crying of people, the howling
and barking of dogs, the noise and clattering of armours.
Of all this have I been the cause. Even this day I have
clothed the knights of this city in mourning. I have left
servants destitute of a master. And because you stand
amazed at the sound of my crimes I will open the business
unto you. It is now many days, dear father, since a gentleman called Calisto, whom you knew, did pine away for my
love. (As for his virtues, they were generally known.) So
great was his love-torment that he was driven to reveal his
passion to a crafty woman named Celestina, which Celestina
drew my secret from my bosom and made the match between us. Overcome with the love of Calisto, I gave him
entrance to your house; he scaled your walls with ladders,
brake into your garden, and took the flower of my virginity.
Almost a month have we lived in this delightful error of
love. And when he came last night unto me, e'en just about
the time that he should have returned home, as Fortune
would have it, the walls being high, the night dark, the
ladder light and weak, his servants unacquainted with that
kind of service, he going down hastily to see a fray in the
street, being in choler, making more haste than good speed,
not eyeing well his steps, he set his foot quite beside the
rungs, and so fell down. With that unfortunate fall, he
pitched upon his head and had his brains dashed in pieces
against the stones of the street. Thus did the Destinies cut
off his thread, cut off my hope, cut off my glory. What
cruelty were it now in me that I should live all the days of

my life! His death inviteth mine. Inviteth? Nay, enforceth. It teacheth that I also should fall headlong down that I may imitate him in all things. Calisto, I come! My best-beloved father, I beseech you that our obsequies be solemnized together and that we may both be interred in one tomb. Recommend me to my most dear mother, and inform her of the doleful occasion of my death. I am glad with all my heart that she is not here with you. I sorrow much for myself, more for you, but most for her. God be with you and her. To Him I offer up my soul. Do you cover up this body that now cometh down.

She throws herself from the tower.

PLEBERIO'S *house*

PLEBERIO, ALISA

ALISA. Pleberio, my lord, why do you weep?

PLEBERIO. Our solace is in the suds, our joy is turned into annoy, let us no longer desire to live! Behold her whom thou broughtest forth and I begot—broken to pieces! O my dear wife, rise up, and if any life be left in thee, spend it with me in tears and lamentation! Hard heart of a father, why dost thou not burst to see thyself bereavèd of thy heir? For whom didst thou build those turrets, for whom planted trees, for whom wrought ships? O variable Fortune, stewardess of temporal happiness, why didst thou not execute thy cruel anger against me? Thou mightest, O Fortune, fluctuant as thou art, have given me a sorrowful youth and a mirthful age, neither have therein perverted order. O World, World, in my more tender years I thought thou wast ruled by reason, but now thou seemest unto me a labyrinth of errors; an habitation of wild beasts; a dance full of changes; a fen full of mire; a steep and craggy mountain; a meadow full of snakes; a garden pleasant to look at but without fruit. O thou false World! Thou dost put out our eyes and then to make amends anointest the place with oil; after thou hast done us harm, thou givest us cold comfort, saying that it is some ease to the miserable to have companions in misery. But I, alas, disconsolate old man, stand all alone. I am singular in sorrow; no misfortune is like unto mine. What remedy now, thou flattering World, wilt thou afford my age? Who shall cherish me, who with gentle usage shall cocker my decaying years? O Love, Love, what end have thy servants had? As also that false bawd Celestina who died by the hands of the faithfullest companions that ever she lighted upon! They lost their heads; Calisto, he brake his neck; and my daughter——! Some, O Love, have called thee a god, but I would have such fools consider—it savours not of a deity to murder those that follow him. Thou enemy to all reason! Thy fire is of lightning which scorches unto death! The sticks which thy flames consume are the souls and lives of numberless human creatures, not Christians only, but Gentiles and Jews. What service did Paris do thee? What Helena? What Clytemnestra? What Aegisthus? And all the World knows how it went with them. I complain of the World because I was bred up in it. For had not the World given me life, I had not therein begot Melibea. Not being begot, she had not been born. Not being born, I had not loved her. And not loving her, I should not have mourned, as now I do. O my bruised daughter, why hast thou left me comfortless and all alone in this vale of tears?

CELESTINA (first version published in 1499) has been published in four English translations: James Mabbe's (1631), Lesley Byrd Simpson's (1955), Mack Hendricks Singleton's (1958), and Phyllis Hartnoll's (1959). Mabbe's text stands to the later ones as the King James Bible stands to the several twentieth-century versions of holy writ: modern scholars, as it seems to the present editor, cannot make up in accuracy for what they lose in poetry and wit.

For this reason, Mabbe's text is the basis of the stage version published here. A few obsolete words have been replaced by familiar ones. Brief, bridging passages were written in when the cuts made them necessary. But Mabbe's words were seriously interfered with by the modern adaptor only where Mabbe had replaced the Catholic nomenclature of the Spanish with pagan nomenclature. In order, no doubt, to avoid religious controversy, Mabbe made Rojas' characters visit a "myrtle grove" and pray to "Jove" where the Spanish bluntly said St. Mary Magdalen's Church and God. There was obviously no need to conceal Rojas' anti-clericalism in the year 1959.

A number of English stage versions of *Celestina* have preceded the present one. The most famous of these, an early sixteenth-century "Interlude," was reprinted with the Mabbe text in the Broadway Translations. Another anonymous stage adaptation, this one much closer to the original, was published in London in 1707, a copy being preserved in Columbia University Library. At least two English-language productions of a shortened *Celestina* have been reported in the nineteen-fifties: one in a text prepared by Mack Hendricks Singleton at the University of Wisconsin, the other, based on Mabbe, at Joan Littlewood's Theatre Workshop in East London. Neither of these adaptations has been available for inspection, nor has the recent Spanish adaptation, successfully produced at the Eslava Theatre in Madrid and taken to the International Festival in Paris.

There is one important study of *Celestina* in English: *The Art of La Celestina,* by Stephen Gilman (Madison, Wisconsin, 1956).

SCAPIN
and
DON JUAN
by Molière
Translated by Albert Bermel

In one of Molière's most popular plays, Scapin, that monarch of con men, puts his endless store of ingenuity to work, getting two lovesick young men married to the girls they pine for and, along the way, taking revenge on their grasping old fathers.

Closed down after its first, highly successful run because of opposition from powerful enemies of the playwright, *Don Juan* was performed in a bowdlerized version for almost two hundred years, until actors, directors and critics restored the original text, recognizing it as the most ambitious and mightiest of Molière's prose plays

paper • ISBN: 0-936839-80-5

APPLAUSE

CLASSICAL TRAGEDY: GREEK & ROMAN

edited byRobert W. Corrigan

"Essential plays in highly readable translations ... useful in any course whose goal is to acquaint students with the masterpieces of Greece and Rome."
Harold Nichols
Author, *The Status of Theatre Research*
Kansas State University

"Outstanding essays ... with the right plays ... I am recommending them for our own Freshman Studies Program."
E. Peter Sargent
Associate Dean, Webster University

"Each play is preceded by an insightful introduction ... carefully compiled anthologies."
Jed H. Davis
Editor, *Theatre Education: Mandate for Tomorrow*
Dean, College of Fellows of the American Theater

"Compelling ... offers a rich variety of translation-voices. ... The essays are unerringly chosen for their variety of critical approaches, accessibility, and potential to stimulate discussion and further reflection."
Felicia Londré
Author, *Tennessee Williams*
University of Missouri

"Corrigan remains one of our most visionary critics of dramatic literature ... [He] demonstrates his genius ... for finding the right critical commentaries to encourage students to discover the true classic nature of these plays."
Douglas C. Sprigg
Chair of Theatre & Film Dept.
Middlebury College

Paper • ISBN: 1-55783-046-0

CLASSICAL COMEDY: GREEK AND ROMAN

edited by Robert W. Corrigan

"The price is right! ... provides serious depth ... excellent choice of plays ... greatly enhanced by critical essays."

Phillip G. Hill
Editor, Our Dramatic Heritage
Furman University

"I know of no other collection of Greek and Roman plays ... as valuable to college and university theatre departments."

James M. Symons
Chair, Theatre Dept, University of Colorado
President, Association for Theatre in Higher Education

"An excellent selection of exciting translations ..."

Arthur W. Bloom
Dean, College of Communication
Loyola Marymount University

"Top of the line! Top notch! Corrigan has done it again! An excellent introduction to Greek and Roman drama."

Christian H. Moe
Chair, Theatre Dept.
Southern Illinois University

"Excellent addition to any freshman humanities syllabus. ... solid foundation for an introductory theatre course."

W.B. Worthen
Dept. of English, University of Texas-Austin

"Splendidly useful...up to Corrigan's usual high standards."

Robert Benedetti
California Institute of Arts
Author, *Actor at Work* (4th Ed.)

Paper • ISBN: 0-936839-85-6

SEEDS OF MODERN DRAMA

Introduced and Edited
by Norris Houghton

Five great forces—Chekhov, Hauptmann, Ibsen, Strindberg, and Zola—dramatists whose works define, embrace and transcend the trends and genres of the modern stage, meet here in this extraordinary exhibition of their sustained and sustaining power in today's theatre.

The ideal text for any course venturing into modern drama, Norris Houghton's volume boasts five landmark plays in distinguished modern translations.

THERESE RAQUIN
Zola

AN ENEMY OF THE PEOPLE
Ibsen

MISS JULIE
Strindberg

THE WEAVERS
Hauptmann

THE SEA GULL
Chekhov

Paper • ISBN: 0-936839-15-5

THE LIFE OF THE DRAMA
by Eric Bentley

" ... Eric Bentley's radical new look at the grammar of theatre ... is a work of exceptional virtue, and readers who find more in it to disagree with than I do will still, I think, want to call it central, indispensable. ... The book justifies its title by being precisely about the ways in which life manifests itself in the theatre. ... If you see any crucial interest in such topics as the death of Cordelia, Godot's non-arrival ... this is a book to be read and read again."

—Frank Kermode
THE NEW YORK REVIEW OF BOOKS

"The Life of the Drama ... is a remarkable exploration of the roots and bases of dramatic art, the most far-reaching and revelatory we have had."

—Richard Gilman
BOOK WEEK

"The Life of the Drama is Eric Bentley's magnum opus or to put it more modestly his best book. I might call it an esthetic of the drama, but this again sounds ponderous; the book is eminently lucid and often helpfully epigrammatic. Everyone genuinely interested in the theatre should read it. It is full of remarkable insights into many of the most important plays ever written."

—Harold Clurman

paper • ISBN: 1-55783-110-6

MEDIEVAL AND TUDOR DRAMA
TWENTY-FOUR PLAYS
Edited and with Introductions
by John Gassner

The rich tapestry of medieval belief, morality and manners shines through this comprehensive anthology of the twenty-four major plays that bridge the dramatic worlds of medieval and Tudor England. Here are the plays that paved the way to the Renaissance and Shakespeare. In John Gassner's extensively annotated collection, the plays regain their timeless appeal and display their truly international character and influence.

Medieval and Tudor Drama remains the indispensable chronicle of a dramatic heritage — the classical plays of Hrotsvitha, folk and ritual drama, the passion play, the great morality play *Everyman*, the Interlude, Tudor comedies *Ralph Roister Doister* and *Gammer Gurton's Needle*, and the most famous of Tudor tragedies, *Gorboduc*. The texts have been modernized for today's readers and those composed in Latin have been translated into English.

paper • ISBN: 0-936839-84-8

BLACK HEROES

SEVEN PLAYS

Edited, with an Introduction, by Errol Hill

Some of America's most outstanding playwrights of the last two centuries have catapulted the lives of legendary black men and women out of the history books and onto the stage. Errol Hill has collected the most resonant of these powerful examples in *Black Heroes* where we meet Nat Turner, Frederick Douglass, Harriet Tubman, Martin Luther King, Paul Robeson, Marcus Garvey and Jean Jacques Dessaline.

EMPEROR OF HAITI
Langston Hughes

NAT TURNER
Randolph Edmonds

HARRIET TUBMAN
May Miller

IN SPLENDID ERROR
William Branch

I, MARCUS GARVEY
Edgar White

PAUL ROBESON
Phillip Hayes Dean

ROADS OF THE MOUNTAIN TOP
Ron Milner

paper • ISBN: 1-55783-027-4

THE MISER and GEORGE DANDIN
by Molière
Translated by Albert Bermel

Harpagon, the most desperate, scheming miser in literature, starves his servants, declines to pay them, cheats his own children if he can save (or make) a few coins, and when his hoard of gold disappears, insanely accuses himself of being the thief.

Dandin, in this rousing classic, not previously available in English for sixty years, is a man in a plight that everybody but him will find entertaining.

paper • ISBN: 0-936839-75-9

THE DOCTOR IN SPITE OF HIMSELF
and THE BOURGEOIS GENTLEMAN
by Molière
Translated by Albert Bermel

In *The Doctor in Spite of Himself*, Molière's scalpel-sharp satire of the medical profession, Sganarelle's wife spreads the word that he is secretly a brilliant doctor who won't reveal his skills unless he is unmercifully punished.

Bourgeois Gentleman, Molière's classic treatment of snobbery, presents Monsieur Jourdain's obsessive desire to move up out of the ranks of the middle class and associate with the gentry.

paper • ISBN: 0-936839-77-5

THE THREE CUCKOLDS
by Leon Katz

"They loved him in Venice and Rome, and Verona, and Padua. That was 400 years ago, but they also love him NOW! Arlecchino, chief clown and scapegoat of commedia dell'arte comedy makes a triumphal comeback in *The Three Cuckolds!*"
—LOS ANGELES TIMES

paper • ISBN: 0-936839-06-6

THE SON OF ARLECCHINO
by Leon Katz

Watch out! CAUTION! Arlecchino and his band of madcaps are leaping out of centuries of retirement. They're fed up with being shoved around like second-rate citizens of the stage. Their revolt is led by none other than the champion of present day commedia, Leon Katz, who incites the troupe to perform all their most famous zany routines.

paper • ISBN: 0-936839-07-4

CELESTINA
by Fernando de Rojas
Adapted by Eric Bentley • Translated by James Mabbe

The central situation is a simple one: a dirty old woman is helping a courtly young gentleman to seduce a girl. The wonder of the thing lies in the art with which de Rojas derives a towering tragedy — or rather tragi-comedy.

paper • ISBN: 0-936839-01-5

THE PREGNANT PAUSE or LOVE'S LABOR LOST
by Georges Feydeau

Hector Ennepèque, first-time father-to-be, is in extended labor and protracted comic convulsions over his wife Léonie's imminent delivery. A brilliant tableau of conjugal chaos by the master of the genre.

paper • ISBN: 0-936839-58-9

A SLAP IN THE FARCE and A MATTER OF WIFE AND DEATH
by Eugene Labiche

An accidental grope on a dimly lit bus earns for the painter, Antoine, a slap whose force resounds around Labiche's wildly comic labyrinth, from which there is no escape, except, alas, for (what else?) romance and marriage.

paper • ISBN: 0-936839-82-1

THE BRAZILIAN
by Henri Meilhac and Ludovic Halèvy

Two amorous actresses are out to capture the affections of a wealthy Paris producer. The play's mad improvisation is a romp in the best tradition of door-slamming French bedroom farce.

❀APPLAUSE❀

LIFE IS A DREAM
AND OTHER SPANISH CLASSICS
Edited by Eric Bentley
Translated by Roy Campbell

"The name of Eric Bentley is enough to guarantee the significance of any book of or about drama."

—Robert Penn Warren

LIFE IS A DREAM
by Calderon de la Barca

FUENTE OVEJUNA
by Lope de Vega

THE TRICKSTER OF SEVILLE
by Tirso de Molina

THE SIEGE OF NUMANTIA
by Miguel de Cervantes

paper • ISBN: 1-55783-006-1   cloth • ISBN: 1-55783-005-3

THE MISANTHROPE
AND OTHER FRENCH CLASSICS
Edited by Eric Bentley

"I would recommend Eric Bentley's collection to all who really care for theatre."

—Harold Clurman

THE MISANTHROPE
by Molière
English version by Richard Wilbur

PHAEDRA
by Racine
English version by Robert Lowell

THE CID
by Corneille
English version by James Schevill

FIGARO'S MARRIAGE
by Beaumarchais
English version by Jacques Barzun

paper • ISBN: 0-936839-19-8

ANTIGONE
by Bertolt Brecht
A Play —With selections from Brecht's Model Book
Translated by Judith Malina

Sophocles, Hölderlin, Brecht, Malina — four major figures in the world's theatre — they have all left their imprint on this remarkable dramatic text. Friedrich Hölderlin translated Sophocles into German, Brecht adapted Hölderlin, and now Judith Malina has rendered Brecht's version into a stunning English incarnation.

Brecht's *Antigone* is destined to be performed, read and discussed across the English-speaking world.

paper • ISBN: 0-936839-25-2

MARY STUART
by Friedrich Schiller

Adapted by Eric Bentley
Translated by Joseph Mellish

Many have told the tragic tales of Mary Queen of Scots but none more powerfully than Friedrich Schiller. Powerful is the word for, as Schiller himself put it:

"[Mary] does not feel or excite tenderness. It is her destiny to experience and enflame violent passions."

Eric Bentley's lean, forceful rendering of the German masterpiece will command the attention of theatre audiences for many years to come.

paper • ISBN: 0-936839-00-7

APPLAUSE

ELIZABETHAN DRAMA
Eight Plays
Edited and with Introductions by
John Gassner and William Green

Boisterous and unrestrained like the age itself, the Elizabethan theatre has long defended its place at the apex of English dramatic history. Shakespeare was but the brightest star in this extraordinary galaxy of playwrights. Led by a group of young playwrights dubbed "the university wits," the Elizabethan popular stage was imbued with a dynamic force never since equalled. The stage boasted a rich and varied repertoire from courtly and romantic comedy to domestic and high tragedy, melodrama, farce, and histories. The Gassner-Green anthology revives the whole range of this universal stage, offering us the unbounded theatrical inventiveness of the age.

Arden of Feversham, **Anonymous**

The Spanish Tragedy, by **Thomas Kyd**

Friar Bacon and Friar Bungay, by **Robert Greene**

Doctor Faustus, by **Christopher Marlowe**

Edward II, by **Christopher Marlowe**

Everyman in His Humour, by **Ben Jonson**

The Shoemaker's Holiday, by **Thomas Dekker**

A Woman Killed with Kindness, by **Thomas Heywood**

paper • ISBN: 1-55783-028-2